HOW TO STOP BEING TOXIC

UNLOCK THE POWER OF SELF-AWARENESS TO BREAK MANIPULATIVE HABITS AND BUILD GENUINE RELATIONSHIPS

JACKSON PORTER

TABLE OF CONTENTS

PART THREE
BUILDING GENUINE RELATIONSHIPS WITH OTHERS

INTRODUCTION

Have you ever found yourself trapped in a cycle of toxicity, unable to break free? Have you felt the weight of your manipulative tendencies dragging you down, straining your relationships, and leaving you feeling isolated and alone?

Two years ago, I found myself at rock bottom, consumed by jealousy, self-centeredness, and a deep-rooted fear of abandonment. My toxic behaviors were pushing away the people I cared about most, leaving me feeling more isolated than ever. It was a dark and lonely place, but it was also the catalyst for change.

In the depths of my despair, I made a decision—a decision to confront my demons head-on and embark on a journey of self-discovery and transformation. It wasn't easy, and it certainly wasn't comfortable, but it was necessary. And let me tell you, it was worth it.

As I stumbled through the darkness of my own toxic behaviors, I recognized the necessity for a method that would establish the groundwork for enduring transformation. That's when I developed the Anti-Toxic SSB system.

This system, born out of my own journey of trial and error, is a framework for overcoming toxic behaviors and nurturing healthy, genuine relationships. It's not a one-size-fits-all solution but rather a flexible and adaptable approach that can be tailored to fit your unique circumstances and challenges.

At its core, the Anti-Toxic SSB system is built on three key pillars: self-awareness, self-love, and building genuine connections.

Self-awareness is the foundation upon which true transformation is built. It's about taking a long, hard look in the mirror and acknowledging the parts of ourselves that we'd rather keep hidden. It's about recognizing our toxic behaviors and patterns and understanding how they impact ourselves and those around us. Through self-reflection and introspection, we can begin to unravel the tangled mess of our own psyche and gain clarity on the path forward.

But self-awareness is just the beginning. The next step is **self-love**—perhaps the most challenging and yet the most essential aspect of the journey. Self-love is about embracing ourselves, flaws and all, and recognizing our inherent worth and value as human beings. It's about treating ourselves with kindness, compassion, and respect and learning to forgive ourselves for our past mistakes. And it's about setting boundaries and prioritizing our own well-being, even when it feels uncomfortable or unfamiliar.

Finally, **building genuine connections** is about cultivating meaningful relationships based on trust, respect, and mutual understanding. It's about letting go of the need to control or manipulate others and instead embracing vulnerability and authenticity in our interactions. It's about showing up fully and genuinely in our relationships and allowing ourselves and others to be seen and accepted for who we truly are.

These three pillars will provide a guiding system and the necessary tools for personal transformation. Achieving the goals of self-awareness, self-love, and building genuine connections can feel overwhelming and daunting. However, with the support of these pillars, we can navigate through the challenges and complexities of our journey towards growth and authenticity. That's why I'm committed to providing you with practical strategies, insightful guidance, and unwavering support throughout this journey.

This book isn't just for those who fit the textbook definition of a narcissist. It's for anyone who has taken a hard look at themselves and recognized toxic traits in their behavior. Whether you've struggled with communication issues, boundary-setting, or any other toxic behavior, this book is here to guide you toward a healthier, more fulfilling way of living.

By acknowledging and addressing these toxic behaviors, you're not just benefiting yourself but also the people around you. Improving yourself is about creating stronger, more positive relationships and fostering a better environment for everyone involved.

I know what it's like to push people away with self-centered behaviors and to crave validation that I never seemed to find. I know the toll that negativity can take on your relationships and the strain it puts on even the closest bonds. I know the endless cycle of self-hatred and destructive habits, the desperate search for something—anything—to fill the void inside.

But here's the thing—you're not alone.

In fact, you're in the company of many who have experienced the same struggles, me included. We've felt the weight of our toxic behaviors dragging us down, straining our relationships, and leaving us feeling isolated and alone. But we've also found a way out, and I'm here to show you how.

In this book, you will learn to recognize toxic behavior patterns and how to intercept them before they take hold. You'll gain insight into responding thoughtfully to triggering situations, breaking free from reactive defaults. You'll discover strategies to boost self-confidence and foster a sense of independence, empowering you to navigate life with conviction. Moreover, you'll uncover the keys to rebuilding trust in relationships through transparency and genuine investment. Rooted in your foundational values, these lessons will pave the way for lasting self-improvement, guiding you through challenges and refining your resilience. Embracing the refiner's fire, you'll confront guilt and uncomfortable truths, emerging stronger and more capable of shaping the life you desire.

Picture this—you wake up one morning feeling lighter than you have in years. The weight of guilt and shame has lifted, replaced by a sense of freedom and relief. Looking in the mirror, you see strength and beauty reflected back at you instead of flaws and imperfections.

As you go about your day, you notice a subtle yet profound change in your interactions with others. Where there was once tension and conflict, there is now understanding and empathy. You communicate openly and honestly, free from manipulation or control, and find yourself drawing people in with your warmth and authenticity.

Spending time with loved ones is joyful and fulfilling, without fear or insecurity clouding the experience. You genuinely celebrate their happiness and success, finding validation from within rather than seeking it from external sources.

With each passing day, you continue to grow and evolve, embracing challenges as opportunities for growth. Navigating life's ups and downs with grace and resilience, you feel confident in your ability to overcome obstacles.

Looking back on your journey, you marvel at how far you've come. From the grips of toxicity, you've emerged as a beacon of love and genuine connection. Each step forward has been a lesson learned, and every mistake is a stepping stone toward growth.

As you gaze toward the future, it's filled with endless possibilities, a testament to your resilience and unwavering determination.

This is the promise of redemption that awaits you at the end of this journey. It won't be easy, and it won't happen overnight. But with courage, determination, and a willingness to confront your demons head-on, you can emerge from the darkness into the light.

Together, let's break free from the bonds of toxicity and embrace a life filled with love, authenticity, and genuine connection. The journey will be difficult, but I promise you, it will be worth it. So, are you ready to take the first step? Let's do this.

PART ONE
SELF-AWARENESS

Everything that irritates us about others can lead us to an understanding of ourselves.

CARL GUSTAV JUNG

In this opening segment of our book, we embark on a journey together to dive into the cornerstone of our Anti-Toxic SSB System—self-awareness. Here, we urge you to confront your own experiences and insights head-on, challenging you to delve deeper into understanding yourself. By embracing this journey of self-discovery, you'll equip yourself with the essential tools to identify toxic patterns and pave the way for transformative change in your relationships and daily life. Self-awareness isn't just the first step; it's the crucial foundation upon which meaningful progress is built. It's about confronting uncomfortable truths about ourselves and acknowledging our shortcomings so we can chart a course toward personal growth and fulfillment.

CHAPTER 1
ARE YOU TOXIC?

I used to believe I was immune to toxic behavior, but one incident shattered that illusion, leaving me to confront the harsh reality of my own harmful tendencies.

It all began innocently enough, or so I thought. Growing up, I prided myself on being a good friend and partner. Yet, there was an underlying current of insecurity and fear of abandonment that I never acknowledged. It wasn't until my relationship with my best friend, Aaron, reached a breaking point that I was forced to confront my toxic behavior.

Aaron and I had been inseparable since childhood. We shared everything, from secrets to dreams, and I believed our bond was unbreakable. However, as we grew older, tensions began to simmer beneath the surface. I couldn't understand why Aaron seemed distant and aloof, and I grew increasingly resentful of his apparent indifference.

One fateful evening, fueled by frustration and hurt, I lashed out at Aaron during a heated argument. My words were sharp and cutting, aimed at wounding. At that moment, I didn't realize the damage I was inflicting, blinded by my own pain.

The fallout was swift and brutal. Aaron distanced himself from me, leaving me to grapple with the wreckage of our friendship. Once I finally reflected on our relationship, I recognized the toxic patterns I had perpetuated. My need for validation and fear of rejection had driven me to manipulate and control, ultimately pushing away the person I cared about most.

The realization was a harsh wake-up call. I had always prided myself on being a good friend, yet I had failed to see the toxic behaviors lurking within me. The pain of losing Aaron forced me to confront those demons head-on, igniting a journey of self-discovery and growth.

As I dove deeper into understanding my own toxic tendencies, I vowed to change. It wasn't easy; there were setbacks along the way, but with each step forward, I felt lighter, unburdened by the weight of my past mistakes.

This chapter serves as a powerful reminder that self-awareness is the first step toward personal growth and transformation. Through reflection and introspection, you have the opportunity to recognize and address any toxic tendencies that may be holding you back.

NARCISSISM

Most definitely, we've all heard this word thrown around, and perhaps we do not pay much attention to it. Worse still, some of us may not realize that we are narcissists. It is important that we understand the true meaning and implications of narcissism, as it can deeply impact our relationships and overall well-being.

Narcissistic personality disorder (NPD) is a mental health condition characterized by a pervasive pattern of grandiosity, a constant need for admiration, and a lack of empathy for others. People with NPD typically have difficulty maintaining healthy relationships, as they tend to prioritize their own desires and disregard the feelings and needs of others. They may also have fragile self-esteem, which can lead to intense reactions to criticism or perceived slights (Mitra & Fluyau, 2023).

Recognizing toxic traits within ourselves can be uncomfortable and challenging, but it is a vital step toward personal growth and healing. By acknowledging and addressing these tendencies, we can cultivate healthier relationships, improve our emotional intelligence, and foster greater empathy toward others. This book is for anyone grappling with toxic habits or traits, not solely those with NPD. By exploring the symptoms and causes of NPD, we may gain insight into where our own toxic behaviors originated. It's important to note that diagnosing NPD requires a thorough evaluation by a mental health professional. This book does not aim to diagnose NPD but offers strategies to individuals seeking to overcome any narcissistic traits they've developed, whether or not they have NPD.

Signs and Symptoms of NPD

Self-awareness demands that we recognize the signs and symptoms that we may be narcissists. Understanding these indicators is crucial for fostering personal growth and healthier relationships. Below, we look into the details of NPD, shedding light on its key signs and symptoms:

Grandiosity—Individuals with NPD often have an exaggerated sense of self-importance. They may believe they are unique, special, or superior to others. This grandiose self-view may lead them to constantly seek admiration and validation from others.

Lack of Empathy—Empathy, or the ability to understand and share the feelings of others, is often lacking in individuals with NPD. They may struggle to recognize or empathize with the emotions and experiences of those around them, leading to difficulties in forming meaningful relationships.

Sense of Entitlement—Individuals with NPD often feel entitled to special treatment and privileges. They may expect others to cater to their needs and desires without considering the needs of others.

Exploitative Behavior—Narcissists may exploit others to achieve their own goals or satisfy their own needs. This can manifest in manipulative or abusive behavior in relationships, as they prioritize their own interests above those of others.

Fragile Self-Esteem—Despite their outward displays of confidence and superiority, individuals with NPD often have fragile self-esteem. They may react strongly to criticism or perceived slights, becoming defensive or hostile in response.

Difficulty Maintaining Relationships—Due to their egocentric worldview and lack of empathy, narcissists often struggle to maintain healthy, long-lasting relationships. Their behavior may push others away, leaving them to feel isolated or misunderstood.

Causes and Risk Factors of Narcissism

If someone genuinely intends good in their life, it's reasonable to assume they wouldn't want to be diagnosed with Narcissistic Personality Disorder (NPD). It's important to recognize that some, if not most, of us who present with NPD do so because of issues or factors beyond our control. Understanding the causes and risk factors of narcissism can shed light on the complexities of this condition and pave the way for greater empathy and support for individuals struggling with NPD.

Narcissism can develop from a combination of genetic, environmental, and psychological factors (Gillihan, 2022). Understanding these causes and risk factors provides insight into the development of narcissistic personality traits.

- **Genetics**—Some research suggests that genetics may play a role in the development of narcissism. Individuals with a family history of narcissism or other personality disorders may be at a higher risk of developing narcissistic traits themselves (Green, 2023).

- **Parental Influence**—The way a person is raised significantly impacts the development of narcissistic traits. Children who are excessively praised or indulged by their parents may grow up with an inflated sense of self-importance and entitlement. Conversely, children who are neglected or emotionally abused may develop narcissistic traits as a defense mechanism to cope with feelings of inadequacy.
- **Environmental Factors**—Certain environmental factors, such as societal pressures or cultural norms, can contribute to the development of narcissistic traits. For example, living in a culture that values individualism and success at any cost may encourage narcissistic behavior.
- **Trauma or Adversity**—Experiencing trauma or adversity during childhood or adolescence can also contribute to the development of narcissistic traits. Individuals who have experienced abuse, neglect, or other forms of trauma may develop narcissistic defenses to protect themselves from further harm.
- **Personality Traits**—Certain personality traits, such as low self-esteem or a fragile sense of self, may predispose individuals to develop narcissistic tendencies. Additionally, individuals with certain personality disorders, such as borderline personality disorder or antisocial personality disorder, may also exhibit narcissistic traits.

- **Cultural Influences**—Cultural factors can also influence the development of narcissism. For example, living in a society that values material wealth, status, and appearance may promote narcissistic behavior as individuals strive to meet societal expectations and gain validation from others.
- **Social Media and Technology**—The rise of social media and technology has created new opportunities for narcissistic behavior. Platforms like Instagram and Facebook provide a stage for individuals to showcase their accomplishments and seek validation from others, which can reinforce narcissistic tendencies.

Overall, narcissism is a complex phenomenon influenced by a variety of factors. When we understand the causes and risk factors of narcissism, we can gain insight into our behavior and take steps toward personal growth and self-awareness.

Covert Narcissism

Covert narcissism is a subtype of NPD characterized by a more subtle and inwardly focused expression of narcissistic traits.

Individuals with covert narcissism often appear modest and self-effacing on the surface, but underneath this facade lies a deep-seated sense of entitlement, insecurity, and a need for validation. They may harbor feelings of envy and resentment toward others whom they perceive as more successful or admired. Instead of openly seeking attention and admiration like their overt counterparts, covert narcissists may manipulate situations and relationships to garner validation indirectly.

Below are some common characteristics of covert narcissism:

- **Hypersensitivity to Criticism**—Covert narcissists may react strongly to criticism or perceived slights, often taking criticism personally and becoming defensive or resentful.
- **Victim Mentality**—They may adopt a victim mentality, portraying themselves as misunderstood or mistreated by others while secretly harboring feelings of superiority.
- **Manipulative Behavior**—Covert narcissists may use manipulation and passive-aggressive tactics to control others and maintain a sense of power and superiority.
- **Lack of Empathy**—Similar to overt narcissists, covert narcissists often lack empathy and may struggle to understand or acknowledge the feelings and perspectives of others.
- **Self-Deception**—Covert narcissists may engage in self-deception, convincing themselves that they are not seeking attention or validation when, in reality, their behaviors are driven by a deep-seated need for admiration.

When to Seek Help for Covert Narcissism

It's important to recognize when the situation with covert narcissism becomes too overwhelming or detrimental to your well-being. Be aware of signs that it may be time to seek professional help.

Imagine you're constantly at odds with your partner, unable to find common ground on even the simplest of issues. Every conversation seems to escalate into an argument, leaving you both feeling frustrated and misunderstood. If this sounds familiar, it could be a sign that professional help is needed to address the underlying issues causing these persistent relationship issues.

Now, picture yourself in a situation where your emotions often feel like they're running rampant. You find yourself consumed by intense feelings of anger, jealousy, or sadness, unable to control or express them in healthy ways. Despite your best efforts, you feel overwhelmed and unable to cope with the overwhelming emotions. Seeking therapy can provide you with the tools and support needed to better manage your emotions and find healthier ways to express yourself.

Consider how your narcissistic behaviors are impacting your work and social life. Perhaps you've noticed that your relationships with colleagues or friends are suffering due to your manipulative or controlling tendencies. Maybe you're struggling to perform at work because your focus is constantly consumed by maintaining a facade of perfection. If your narcissistic behaviors are negatively impacting your overall quality of life, it may be time to seek professional guidance to address these issues.

Now, think about your overall sense of fulfillment and satisfaction in life. Despite achieving success or receiving external validation, you still feel empty or unfulfilled. No matter how much you accomplish, you can't shake the feeling that something is missing.

Take a moment and reflect on your ability to maintain close, meaningful relationships. Do you find yourself struggling to connect with others on a deeper level, often resorting to manipulation or control to maintain relationships? Perhaps you've noticed a pattern of pushing people away or being unable to empathize with their feelings.

Overt Narcissism

Overt narcissism, like covert narcissism, is a subtype of NPD. However, it differs in its presentation and expression of narcissistic traits.

Overt narcissism is characterized by an outwardly grandiose and attention-seeking demeanor. Individuals with overt narcissism often display exaggerated self-importance, a constant need for admiration, and a sense of entitlement. They may openly boast about their achievements, seek validation and admiration from others, and demonstrate a lack of empathy for those around them.

At a place of work, an example of overt narcissism might involve a colleague who constantly seeks attention and admiration from their coworkers. These individuals may frequently boast about their accomplishments, exaggerate their contributions to projects, and openly seek praise and recognition for their work, often at the expense of others. They may dominate meetings, interrupting others and dismissing their ideas in favor of their own. Additionally, they may be dismissive of feedback or criticism, viewing themselves as infallible and superior to their peers. Their behavior creates a toxic work environment characterized by competitiveness, resentment, and a lack of collaboration.

While both overt and covert narcissism share core characteristics of NPD, they differ in their presentation and behavior.

- **Expression of Traits**—Overt narcissists openly display their narcissistic traits, whereas covert narcissists tend to be more subtle and secretive in their behavior.
- **Attention-Seeking**—Overt narcissists actively seek attention and admiration from others, often through grandiose displays and self-promotion. In contrast, covert narcissists may seek validation indirectly, using manipulation or passive-aggressive tactics.
- **Grandiosity**—Overt narcissists often exhibit grandiose fantasies and beliefs about their own superiority, whereas covert narcissists may harbor similar beliefs but keep them hidden beneath a facade of modesty.
- **Empathy**—While both types of narcissists lack empathy, overt narcissists may be more overtly

callous and dismissive of others' feelings, whereas covert narcissists may feign empathy or adopt a victim mentality to manipulate others.

When to Seek Help for Overt Narcissism

Recognizing when to seek help for overt narcissism is crucial for personal growth and well-being. Look for indicators that it may be time to seek professional guidance.

Imagine finding yourself in constant conflict with coworkers, friends, or family members despite your best efforts to maintain healthy relationships. Your narcissistic tendencies seem to strain these connections, leaving you feeling isolated and frustrated. If this resonates with you, it might be time to seek support to navigate and improve these important relationships.

Picture yourself at work, struggling to collaborate with colleagues, receive feedback, or manage conflicts due to your narcissistic behaviors. Despite your skills and talents, your interactions with others are hindered by your need for control or validation. Seeking professional guidance can equip you with the interpersonal skills needed to thrive in your professional environment.

Now, consider your emotional state. Despite outward displays of confidence, you find yourself grappling with feelings of emptiness, loneliness, or dissatisfaction. Your narcissism may provide a facade of superiority, but beneath it lies a deep sense of discontent. Seeking help from a therapist or counselor can help you explore these underlying issues and cultivate greater emotional well-being.

Reflect on any legal or personal consequences that may have arisen from your narcissistic behavior. Perhaps conflicts with authorities or legal action from others have prompted you to reconsider your actions. Seeking help can assist you in addressing the root causes of your behavior and developing healthier coping mechanisms to prevent further harm.

SIGNS YOU'RE TOXIC

Some time ago, during a gathering with friends, I experienced a profound realization. Despite having used the term "toxic" to describe others before, I couldn't confidently pinpoint what behaviors constituted toxicity. As we engaged in conversation, one friend mentioned their toxic team leader, sparking my curiosity. While others nodded in agreement, I found myself fixated on the topic, questioning what it truly meant to be toxic. Reflecting on this experience, I realized the importance of identifying the signs of toxic behavior.

Dismissive Advice—You frequently tell others to "just change" their mindset without considering their individual circumstances or struggles. While positive thinking can be beneficial, dismissing someone's challenges with simplistic advice can be invalidating and unhelpful. It's important to offer support and empathy rather than simplistic solutions.

Forcing Your Beliefs—You frequently impose your own beliefs or opinions onto others, disregarding their perspectives and boundaries. Instead of respecting diverse viewpoints, you insist that your truth is the only valid perspective, which can alienate and frustrate those around you.

Inconsistency—Your behavior and actions often fluctuate unpredictably, causing confusion and instability in relationships. Your inconsistency can lead to mistrust and uncertainty, making it challenging for others to rely on you or feel secure in your presence.

Causing Hurt—You tend to make people feel bad about themselves through your words or actions. Whether intentionally or unintentionally, your behavior undermines others' self-esteem and emotional well-being, creating a toxic and unhealthy dynamic in relationships.

Superiority Complex—You harbor an inflated sense of self-importance and believe that you are inherently better or more deserving than others. This superiority complex manifests in arrogance, condescension, and a lack of empathy toward those you perceive as inferior. Your attitude of superiority can breed resentment and alienation among peers.

Controlling Behavior—You frequently exert control over others, dictating their actions, thoughts, or emotions to suit your own agenda. Your need for control can be suffocating and oppressive, stifling the autonomy and agency of those around you.

Emotional Manipulation—You use emotional manipulation tactics to influence or control others' behavior. Whether through guilt-tripping, gaslighting, or playing the victim, you exploit people's emotions for your own benefit, often at their expense.

Lack of Accountability—You avoid taking responsibility for your actions or their consequences. Instead of owning up to your mistakes, you deflect blame onto others or make excuses to justify your behavior, undermining trust and integrity in relationships.

Passive-Aggressiveness—You express hostility or resentment indirectly, often through subtle digs, sarcasm, or silent treatment. Your passive-aggressive behavior creates tension and conflict in relationships as others struggle to decode your true feelings or intentions.

Exploiting Vulnerability—You prey on people's vulnerabilities for personal gain or amusement. Whether through manipulation, deception, or coercion, you exploit others' weaknesses for your own benefit, disregarding their well-being and dignity.

HOW DOES BEING TOXIC AFFECT YOU?

As we delve deeper into understanding toxic behavior, it's important to recognize the challenges it brings to our lives.

Feeling Isolated—Picture that you've been invited to a group outing with your friends, but your controlling behavior takes center stage. You insist on choosing the venue, dismissing everyone else's suggestions. As a result, your friends feel sidelined and excluded, eventually leading them to distance themselves from you. Despite your longing for connection, your toxic tendencies push people away, leaving you stranded in a sea of loneliness.

Damaging Friendships—Being overly negative can damage friendships and relationships. Constantly criticizing others, gossiping, or focusing on the negative aspects of situations can create a toxic atmosphere, driving friends away and causing rifts in relationships. I recall a time when a coworker was sick and unable to complete their tasks, so I willingly picked up the slack. However, later on, I confronted them with a question like, "Why can't you do the same for me now?" This not only made them feel guilty but also undermined their situation, creating unnecessary tension in our relationship.

Unhealthy Coping Mechanisms—Toxic behavior often stems from unresolved emotional issues and insecurities. Instead of addressing these underlying issues in healthy ways, you may resort to unhealthy coping mechanisms such as substance abuse, self-harm, or avoidance. These behaviors only exacerbate your feelings of self-hatred and perpetuate a cycle of toxicity, further damaging your mental and emotional well-being.

Struggling with Manipulation and Guilt—You find yourself resorting to manipulation tactics to control others or get your way. I once made a friend feel inadequate about having other priorities by remarking, "I guess our friendship isn't as important to you as it is to me." I manipulated their emotions to serve my own agenda without considering the impact of my words on their feelings.

Overwhelming Jealousy—You experience intense feelings of jealousy, which can lead to insecurity and conflict. Scrolling through social media platforms like Facebook, I often found myself diving into a pool of self-loathing and jealousy upon witnessing other people's success stories in fitness and finance. Instead of celebrating their achievements, I unfairly resented them for it, projecting my insecurities onto their accomplishments. This toxic mindset not only fueled my own self-hatred but also poisoned my relationships as I struggled to authentically support those around me.

Lack of Self-Awareness and Inability to Communicate—You struggle to understand how to communicate effectively with others. For instance, I remember a time when my partner and I had a disagreement about household chores. Instead of calmly discussing our preferences and expectations, I found myself becoming defensive and dismissive when my partner brought up their concerns. This led to misunderstandings and arguments, leaving both of us feeling frustrated and disconnected.

HOW DOES BEING TOXIC AFFECT THE PEOPLE AROUND YOU?

Understanding how our actions affect those around us is crucial for fostering healthy relationships and creating a supportive environment. From feelings of isolation and fear to the development of mental health issues, the repercussions of toxicity extend far beyond individual interactions.

Feeling Drained—The emotional and mental toll of toxic behavior can leave those around you feeling depleted. Enduring constant negativity, manipulation, or criticism can exhaust their well-being, leaving them on edge and anticipating your next outburst or manipulation, contributing to feelings of fatigue and burnout.

Feeling Fearful of You—Toxic behavior often generates a climate of intimidation and apprehension. Your actions, characterized by dominance, aggression, or manipulation, instill a sense of unease and trepidation in others. This intimidation stifles communication and discourages individuals from asserting their needs or opinions, perpetuating a cycle of fear and suppression.

Feeling Secluded—The impact of your toxic behavior can lead individuals to feel isolated and marginalized. Through persistent negativity, manipulation, or criticism, you create an environment that feels unwelcoming and unsupportive. Consequently, those affected may withdraw from social interactions and relationships, seeking refuge from the toxicity that permeates your presence.

Developing Mental Health Issues—The repercussions of your toxic behavior extend to the mental health of those affected, potentially precipitating conditions like depression, anxiety, or other psychological disorders. The persistent exposure to toxicity undermines their self-esteem, erodes their sense of self-worth, and amplifies pre-existing mental health struggles.

Feeling Trapped—The toxic dynamics created by your behavior may leave the people around you feeling trapped and powerless. Whether it's due to your manipulative tactics, controlling behavior, or emotional volatility, they may feel unable to escape the toxic cycle and assert their boundaries. This sense of entrapment can lead to feelings of hopelessness, frustration, and despair as they struggle to break free from the toxic influence you exert over their lives.

IMPORTANCE OF SELF-AWARENESS

Toxic behavior can pose significant challenges in our lives and the lives of others, and it underscores the need for us to enhance self-awareness. It is only when we recognize and understand our toxic behaviors that we can begin to address and overcome toxic patterns.

Self-awareness is the ability to recognize and understand one's own thoughts, emotions, motivations, and behaviors. It involves being mindful of our internal experiences and how they influence our actions and interactions with others. Self-awareness allows us to reflect on our strengths, weaknesses, values, and beliefs, enabling us to make conscious choices and navigate life more effectively.

There are two primary types of self-awareness:

1. **Internal Self-Awareness**—This form of self-awareness involves delving into our inner world of thoughts, emotions, and sensations. Through introspection and self-reflection, we uncover the intricacies of our psyche and how they influence

our perceptions and behaviors. Consider a scenario where you're reflecting on a recent argument with a friend. You pause to examine your emotions and thoughts, realizing that your frustration stemmed from feeling unheard rather than the topic itself. This introspection enables you to recognize your underlying emotions and align your actions with your genuine feelings, fostering internal self-awareness.

2. **External Self-Awareness**—Conversely, external self-awareness entails understanding how others perceive us and the ramifications of our conduct on them. By practicing empathy and taking on different perspectives, we grasp how our behavior impacts those around us. Imagine a scenario where you're in a group setting, and you notice a friend looking uncomfortable during your discussion. You pause to consider your tone and realize it may have come across as dismissive. Adjusting your approach, you acknowledge your friend's input, fostering a better understanding of their perspective and enhancing external self-awareness.

Why Self-Awareness and Honesty Are Important to Fix Toxic Behaviors

Self-awareness and honesty are crucial for addressing and overcoming toxic behaviors because they allow us to recognize and acknowledge our negative patterns and their impact on ourselves and others.

Self-awareness is like shining light on our inner thoughts, feelings, and actions. It allows us to take a step back and observe ourselves from a distance, gaining clarity about why we think, feel, and behave the way we do. When we are self-aware, we can recognize when our actions have negative effects on ourselves and others. For example, we might notice patterns of manipulation, where we try to control or influence others for our own benefit. We might also become aware of our tendency toward negativity, constantly focusing on the flaws or shortcomings of ourselves and those around us.

Honesty is like a beacon of truth that guides our interactions and relationships. It's essential because it enables us to confront and acknowledge when we engage in toxic behaviors. When we are honest with ourselves and others about our actions, we take ownership of our behavior and its consequences. This honesty allows us to recognize the harm we may have caused and accept responsibility for our actions.

By being honest about our behaviors and their effects, we demonstrate integrity and accountability. We show that we are willing to face the truth, even when it's uncomfortable or challenging. Honesty opens the door to genuine communication with others. It allows us to have open and transparent conversations about our behavior and its impact. Through honesty, we can apologize sincerely when necessary and express our commitment to making positive changes.

SELF-REFLECTION—ARE YOU TOXIC?

Answer each question honestly by selecting the response that best reflects your thoughts, feelings, and behaviors. Be mindful of your responses and consider how they align with your interactions with others.

1. How do you typically respond when someone disagrees with you?

   a) Respect their perspective and engage in constructive dialogue.
   b) Become defensive and insist on being right.
   c) Dismiss their opinion and belittle their viewpoint.

2. How do you handle conflicts or disagreements with others?

   a) Seek to find a resolution through open communication and compromise.
   b) Avoid confrontation or ignore the issue altogether.
   c) Resort to manipulation, guilt-tripping, or emotional blackmail to get your way.

3. How do you react when someone else succeeds or receives praise?

a) Feel genuinely happy for their accomplishments and offer congratulations.
b) Experience jealousy or resentment toward their success.
c) Minimize their achievements or attempt to undermine their accomplishments.

4. How do you communicate with others during disagreements or arguments?

a) Listen actively, express your thoughts respectfully, and seek understanding.
b) Interrupt, dominate the conversation, or dismiss the other person's perspective.
c) Use insults, sarcasm, or passive-aggressive comments to assert control or belittle the other person.

5. How do you handle criticism or feedback from others?

a) Reflect on the feedback and consider how you can learn and grow from it.
b) Become defensive, deny responsibility, or shift blame onto others.
c) Dismiss the criticism as irrelevant or attack the person giving feedback.

6. How do you respond when someone expresses their feelings or vulnerabilities to you?

a) Offer empathy, support, and validation for their feelings.
b) Dismiss their feelings or downplay their experiences.
c) Use their vulnerabilities against them or exploit their emotions for your own benefit.

7. How do you behave in group settings or social gatherings?

a) Engage in positive and uplifting conversations and show interest in others' perspectives.
b) Dominate conversations or seek attention to validate your self-worth.
c) Gossip, spread rumors, or create drama to manipulate social dynamics.

8. How do you handle boundaries set by others?

a) Respect their boundaries and adjust your behavior accordingly.
b) Disregard their boundaries or attempt to push past them.
c) Manipulate or guilt-trip them into relinquishing their boundaries.

Scoring:

- For each "a" response, give yourself 1 point
- For each "b" response, give yourself 2 points
- For each "c" response, give yourself 3 points

Interpretation:

- 8-14 points—Your responses suggest healthy and respectful behaviors in your interactions with others. Keep up the positive communication and continue to foster healthy relationships.
- 15-22 points—Your responses indicate some tendencies toward toxic behaviors. Consider reflecting on your interactions with others and explore ways to improve communication and address any underlying issues.
- 23-24 points—Your responses suggest significant toxic behaviors that may be impacting your relationships and well-being. It may be beneficial to seek support from a therapist or counselor to address these patterns and work toward personal growth and change.

Now that you've taken the time to reflect on your behaviors and gain self-awareness of some toxic tendencies, it's important to recognize the progress you've made. In this chapter, we've explored the impact of toxic behavior on ourselves and those around us, highlighting the significance of self-awareness and honesty in addressing these patterns.

By acknowledging our toxic behaviors, we take the first step toward personal growth and positive change.

As we wrap up this chapter, let's remember that self-awareness is a journey, and it's okay to stumble along the way. What matters most is our willingness to confront our behaviors and commit to making positive changes in our lives.

In the next chapter, we'll engage with the process of healing from past hurt that may be contributing to our toxic behavior. This chapter will provide valuable insights and strategies for overcoming emotional wounds and fostering inner healing. Get ready to embark on a journey of self-discovery and transformation as we explore the path to healing and liberation from the chains of our past.

PART TWO
SELF-LOVE

The journey to self-love can be painful, but the fight is worth it.

ANONYMOUS

The journey to self-love can indeed be arduous and fraught with challenges. It demands confronting our deepest insecurities, facing our inner demons, and embracing our flaws with compassion and acceptance. It's a journey that may involve revisiting past wounds, challenging negative beliefs about ourselves, and learning to prioritize our own well-being.

But despite the pain and discomfort it may bring, the fight for self-love is undeniably worth it. It opens the door to profound healing, genuine self-acceptance, and inner peace.

It empowers us to cultivate a deeper connection with ourselves, to honor our needs and desires, and to navigate life with greater resilience and grace.

CHAPTER 2
HEALING FROM THE PAST

When I was younger, there were things that happened to me that I never really healed from. They stayed with me, affecting how I behaved and how I treated others. I carried the weight of those experiences with me everywhere I went, and they colored every aspect of my life.

Growing up, I faced bullying and abuse that left deep scars on my heart. I never fully dealt with the pain and trauma of those experiences. Instead, I buried them deep inside, hoping they would go away on their own. But they didn't. They lingered beneath the surface, shaping my thoughts, feelings, and actions in ways I didn't always understand.

As I got older, I found myself struggling with feelings of inadequacy and worthlessness. I sought validation and acceptance from others, but no matter how much I received, it was never enough. I was always searching for something outside of myself to fill the void within, but nothing ever seemed to work.

It wasn't until I hit rock bottom that I realized I needed to confront my past and heal from the hurt that was holding me back. I couldn't continue living in denial, pretending that everything was okay when it clearly wasn't. I needed to face my demons head-on and find a way to move forward.

And so, I began the journey of healing from my past. It wasn't easy, and it certainly wasn't comfortable, but it was necessary. I sought therapy, surrounded myself with supportive friends and family, and committed myself to the hard work of self-discovery and healing.

Slowly but surely, I started to unravel the tangled mess of my past and make peace with the pain I had experienced. I confronted my demons, forgave those who had hurt me, and learned to love and accept myself for who I truly am. It was a long and difficult road, but with each step forward, I felt a little lighter, a little freer.

Healing from the past isn't a one-time event; it's an ongoing process that requires patience, courage, and perseverance. But as I look back on my journey, I can say with certainty that it was worth it. I may still carry scars from my past, but they no longer define me.

Throughout this chapter, we'll delve deeper into understanding the impact of past hurt on your present behavior and explore practical strategies for healing and moving forward.

ORIGINS OF TOXIC BEHAVIOR

Have you ever lain back and asked yourself, "Why am I toxic? What led me here?"

Several factors could be contributing to your toxic behavior. Let's break them down.

Nature

Your genetic makeup, or what you've inherited from your family, can play a significant role in shaping your behavior. Traits like your temperament, tendencies, and even certain personality traits can be passed down from your parents or ancestors. This means that you might exhibit toxic behaviors similar to those you've observed in your family members.

For instance, if your father had a quick temper and often reacted with anger when things didn't go his way, you might have inherited this trait from him. Growing up in an environment where anger was a common response to challenges, you learned to express your frustrations in the same way. Now, as an adult, you find yourself reacting impulsively and aggressively when faced with difficult situations, just like your father did.

This inheritance of toxic traits isn't limited to just anger. It could manifest in various forms, such as passive-aggressiveness, manipulation, or controlling behavior. Maybe your mother was overly critical or judgmental, and you've internalized these tendencies without even realizing it. As a result, you might find yourself being overly critical of others or struggling to trust those around you, mirroring the behaviors you observed in your family.

Nurture

Your upbringing and the environment you were raised in have a profound influence on your behavior and personality. The experiences and interactions you had during your formative years shaped how you perceive the world and interact with others.

If you grew up in a household marked by constant conflict or where emotions were suppressed or ignored, you might have learned to internalize your feelings or avoid confrontation altogether. In such an environment, expressing emotions openly might have been discouraged or even punished, leading you to struggle with communicating your feelings effectively as an adult.

Additionally, your interactions with caregivers, peers, and other significant figures during childhood can also influence your behavior. I have a close friend who experienced rejection and neglect from caregivers, and they ended up developing feelings of insecurity or mistrust in relationships. These early experiences can shape your attachment style and affect how you form and maintain relationships later in life.

Mental Health Conditions

Certain mental health conditions can significantly influence your behavior and how you interact with others. Conditions such as depression, anxiety, or personality disorders can contribute to toxic behavior in various ways.

For example, individuals struggling with depression may experience feelings of worthlessness or hopelessness, leading them to engage in self-destructive behaviors or lash out at others to cope with their emotional pain. This might manifest as withdrawing from social interactions, expressing negativity, or seeking validation through attention-seeking behaviors.

Similarly, individuals with anxiety disorders may exhibit controlling or manipulative behaviors to alleviate their feelings of insecurity or fear. They may try to exert control over their environment or relationships to reduce their anxiety, even if it means resorting to unhealthy or toxic tactics.

Personality disorders, such as borderline personality disorder or NPD, can also contribute to toxic behavior patterns. For instance, individuals with borderline personality disorder may struggle with intense and unstable emotions, leading to impulsive actions or volatile relationships. On the other hand, individuals with narcissistic personality disorder may exhibit grandiosity, a lack of empathy, and a sense of entitlement, which can result in manipulative or exploitative behavior toward others.

Positive Reinforcement

Our toxic behaviors can sometimes be reinforced by the responses we receive from others or by societal norms. Positive reinforcement occurs when we receive rewards or benefits for engaging in certain behaviors, even if those behaviors are harmful or negative.

For instance, if you're always the center of attention when you gossip or spread rumors, you might continue doing it because it makes you feel powerful or popular. Even though gossiping may hurt others, the attention and validation you receive from those around you can reinforce this behavior.

Similarly, societal norms and cultural influences can contribute to the reinforcement of toxic behaviors. For example, in some social circles or online communities, behaviors like trolling or cyberbullying may be rewarded with attention or approval from peers. This positive feedback can encourage individuals to continue engaging in harmful behaviors, even if they know deep down that it's wrong.

Positive reinforcement creates a cycle where toxic behaviors are repeated and reinforced, leading to further harm to oneself and others. Breaking free from this cycle requires recognizing the negative consequences of our actions and seeking healthier ways to fulfill our needs for validation and belonging.

CAN TRAUMA MAKE YOU TOXIC?

In Chapter 1, we looked into the myriad potential reasons behind toxic behavior. It's essential to recognize that many individuals exhibit toxic behaviors due to unresolved past experiences.

When we discuss the past, it encompasses more than just childhood memories. The past could encompass events from last year, such as being in a toxic relationship or enduring a hostile work environment. Any negative encounter we haven't fully processed and healed from can leave a lasting impact on our psyche.

These unresolved traumas have the power to subtly influence our behavior, often without our conscious awareness. They can shape our perceptions, reactions, and coping mechanisms, leading us to exhibit toxic behaviors in our interactions with others.

For example, if you experienced betrayal or abandonment in a past relationship, you might develop trust issues that manifest as jealousy or possessiveness in your current relationships. Similarly, if you were subjected to emotional abuse or manipulation in the workplace, you might adopt defensive or controlling behaviors as a means of self-protection.

These unresolved traumas can create a cycle of toxic behavior, where our past wounds continue to dictate our present actions. Without addressing and healing from these underlying traumas, we risk perpetuating harmful patterns in our relationships and interactions with others.

How to Know if Your Past Trauma is Affecting You as an Adult

It's important to recognize if past trauma is still affecting you as an adult. Below are some signs to look out for:

- **Flashbacks or Intrusive Memories**—You might experience sudden and intense memories or images of past traumatic events, even when you're not thinking about them. These flashbacks can be distressing and may make you feel like you're reliving the trauma.
- **Avoidance**—You might go out of your way to avoid people, places, or situations that remind you of the trauma. For example, if you were in a car accident, you might avoid driving or being near busy roads.
- **Emotional Numbing**—You might feel emotionally numb or disconnected from others. It may seem like you're going through the motions of life without feeling much joy or excitement.
- **Hyperarousal**—You might feel constantly on edge, irritable, or jumpy. You might have trouble sleeping or concentrating, and you may be easily startled by loud noises or sudden movements.
- **Negative Thoughts and Feelings**—You might have persistent negative thoughts about yourself, others, or the world. You might feel hopeless, guilty, or ashamed, and you may struggle to see a positive future for yourself.
- **Changes in Behavior**—You might notice changes in your behavior, such as increased aggression,

risky behavior, or substance abuse. These behaviors can be coping mechanisms to numb the pain of past trauma.

HOW TO STOP THE BLAME GAME ON PAINFUL ISSUES OF THE PAST

The past may always be a part of us, but it doesn't have to define us. The longer we hold on to what hurt us in the past, the more power we give it to control us and lead us into toxic cycles. In the long run, we end up playing the blame game, where we blame everything, including our behaviors, on the past.

People play the blame game for various reasons.

Avoiding Responsibility—Blaming others or the past allows people to avoid taking responsibility for their actions. It's easier to point fingers at external factors than to acknowledge our role in our own behaviors. This is quite common in a workplace setting; for example, a team member consistently misses deadlines and blames it on their colleagues for not providing necessary information on time. They refuse to take responsibility for their poor time management skills, choosing instead to shift the blame onto others to avoid facing consequences or criticism.

Protecting Self-Esteem—Blaming the past can be a way to protect our self-esteem. Instead of admitting our mistakes or shortcomings, we shift the blame onto something else to maintain a positive self-image. Imagine you're in a relationship that ends badly due to your own actions, such as being emotionally distant or dismissive. Instead of acknowledging your role in the breakup, you blame your partner for not understanding you or for being too demanding. By shifting the blame onto your partner, you protect your self-esteem and avoid facing the uncomfortable truth about your behavior.

Seeking Validation—Some people play the blame game to seek validation or sympathy from others. By portraying themselves as victims of their past, they may garner attention and support from those around them. I recall a coworker who consistently blamed their lack of progress at work on past trauma, such as a difficult upbringing. They often shared their stories with us, hoping to receive sympathy and understanding. By portraying themselves as victims, they sought validation for their struggles and hoped to receive reassurance from us.

Coping with Pain—Blaming the past can also be a way to cope with pain or trauma. It's easier to blame external factors for our struggles than to confront the difficult emotions and memories associated with past experiences. For instance, a person who lost a parent at a young age might blame their current inability to form close relationships on their past loss. Instead of confronting their grief and working through their emotions, they may attribute their struggles to their childhood experiences, avoiding the pain associated with their loss. Blaming the past provides a temporary escape from facing their true emotions and allows them to cope with their pain in a way that feels more manageable.

Maintaining Control—Blaming the past can give people a sense of control over their lives. By attributing their behaviors to external factors, they may feel like they have a justification for their actions and a sense of control over their circumstances. Imagine someone who grew up in a dysfunctional family environment where they experienced neglect and emotional abuse. As an adult, they may blame their toxic behaviors on their upbringing, believing that their past experiences dictate their current actions.

Stay Accountable and Take Responsibility for Your Actions

One of the proven and effective ways that we can stop the blame game is to stay accountable and take responsibility for our actions. Instead of pointing fingers at external factors or the past, acknowledging our role in our behaviors empowers us to make positive changes and break free from toxic cycles.

Taking responsibility means owning up to the things you do and the choices you make. It means recognizing that you have control over your behavior and its consequences. When you take responsibility for your actions, you admit when you've made a mistake and try to make things right.

Why is it important to take responsibility for your actions?

It helps you grow and improve as a person. When you acknowledge your mistakes, you learn from them and can make better choices in the future. Taking responsibility also shows that you respect yourself and others, and it builds trust in your relationships. When you take responsibility, you show that you're reliable and trustworthy, which can help you succeed in life.

Here's how you can take responsibility for your actions:

- **Stop blaming other people.** Instead of pointing fingers at others for your mistakes, recognize your role in what happened.
- **Stop making excuses.** Avoid coming up with reasons why you couldn't have done anything differently. Own up to your actions without trying to justify them.
- **Accept negative emotions.** It's okay to feel bad about something you've done wrong. Acknowledge your feelings, but don't let them excuse your behavior.
- **Act, don't react.** Take proactive steps to make amends or correct the situation rather than simply reacting defensively or impulsively.
- **Practice self-compassion.** Be kind to yourself, even when you've made a mistake. Understand that everyone messes up sometimes, and use it as an opportunity to learn and grow.
- **Take ownership.** Admit when you've done something wrong and take responsibility for the consequences, both to yourself and to others involved.
- **Show remorse for the problem.** Express genuine regret for your actions and the impact they may have had on others.

- **Express gratitude for the reckoning.** Appreciate the opportunity to learn from your mistakes and become a better person as a result.
- **Resolve to take action.** Make a commitment to do better in the future and take concrete steps to prevent similar mistakes from happening again.

How to Stop Defensiveness and Be Open to Feedback

Many of us struggle with receiving criticism. Personally, I used to dread it whenever someone tried to give me constructive feedback. It felt like they were trying to exert power over me, and I didn't like it. Instead of listening, I would often come up with excuses or reasons to justify my actions.

It took me some time to realize that not all feedback is meant to harm or control us. Sometimes, people genuinely want to help us improve. Here are some ways to overcome defensiveness and be more open to feedback:

- **Know your triggers and anticipate them.** Pay attention to situations or topics that tend to trigger defensiveness in you. By recognizing these triggers, you can prepare yourself mentally and emotionally to respond more calmly and constructively when they arise.
- **Give it a name.** Sometimes, simply acknowledging and labeling your defensive reactions can help you gain control over them. Give your defensiveness a name, such as "the inner critic," and remind

yourself that it's just a natural response that you can manage.

- **Assume good intentions**. Instead of automatically assuming that feedback is meant to criticize or attack you, give the other person the benefit of the doubt. Assume that their intentions are positive and that they genuinely want to help you improve.
- **Don't take it personally**. Remember that feedback is about your actions or behavior, not your worth as a person. Try not to take it personally or let it affect your self-esteem. Stay focused on the feedback itself and how you can use it to grow.
- **Listen without reacting**. When someone offers feedback, take a moment to pause and listen without immediately getting defensive. Try to understand their perspective before responding.
- **Practice empathy**. Put yourself in the other person's shoes and try to see things from their point of view. Recognize that they may have valuable insights to offer.
- **Ask for clarification**. If you're unsure about something or need more information, don't hesitate to ask questions. Seek clarification to ensure you fully understand the feedback.
- **Focus on growth**. Instead of seeing feedback as criticism, view it as an opportunity for growth and improvement. Embrace it as a chance to learn and develop your skills.
- **Take ownership**. Acknowledge your mistakes and shortcomings without making excuses. Accept

responsibility for your actions and commit to
making positive changes.

- **Express gratitude**. Thank the person for their
feedback, even if it was difficult to hear. Show
appreciation for their willingness to help you grow.

Forgive Others

Why forgive? Forgiving others can bring peace and freedom
to your life. When you forgive, you let go of anger and
resentment, allowing yourself to move forward without
being weighed down by negative emotions. It's like lifting a
heavy burden off your shoulders and opening yourself up to
new possibilities and happiness. Roberto Assagioli said,
"Without forgiveness, life is governed by . . . an endless cycle
of resentment and retaliation (Menahem & Love, 2013)."

How to Prepare

- **Talk through your feelings**. Take some time to
reflect on how the past hurt you and express your
emotions. Talking to someone you trust can help
you process your feelings and gain clarity.
- **Find the bright side**. Try to look for positive
aspects or lessons that came out of the painful
experience. Finding meaning in the suffering can
make forgiveness easier.
- **Forgive smaller things first**. Start by forgiving
smaller offenses or grievances. Practice forgiving
everyday annoyances or minor conflicts to build
your forgiveness muscle.

Doing the Deed

- **Write a letter**. Consider writing a letter to the person who hurt you, expressing your feelings and your decision to forgive them. You don't have to send the letter; it's more about releasing your emotions and letting go.
- **Share your feelings with someone else**. Talking to a trusted friend or therapist about your forgiveness journey can provide support and encouragement.
- **Look into forgiveness programs**. Explore forgiveness programs or workshops developed by researchers to learn more about forgiveness and gain practical strategies.

Moving On

- **Make good emotional health a lifetime goal**. Prioritize your emotional well-being by practicing self-care, setting boundaries, and seeking support when needed.
- **Work toward your happiness**. Focus on building a fulfilling and joyful life for yourself. Invest in activities and relationships that bring you happiness and fulfillment, and let go of the past that no longer serves you.

HOW TO FORGIVE YOURSELF

It is impossible to heal from the past without forgiving yourself. Forgiving yourself doesn't mean you did something wrong or played a part in what led you there; it means releasing yourself from self-blame and self-criticism. It's about acknowledging that you're human and that everyone makes mistakes. Forgiving yourself allows you to let go of guilt and shame, freeing yourself to move forward with self-compassion and acceptance.

It's okay to acknowledge your mistakes and learn from them, but being overly critical of yourself can hinder your progress. Instead, practice self-compassion and treat yourself with kindness and understanding. Recognize that you are human, and like everyone else, you are prone to making mistakes. Allow yourself to let go of the past and move forward with forgiveness and self-love.

Allow yourself to feel and acknowledge any guilt, regret, or shame without judgment. Recognizing and accepting these emotions is the first step toward healing.

Speak openly about the mistake you made, either to yourself or to a trusted friend or therapist. Articulating your actions can help you confront them directly and take ownership of your past choices.

Shift your perspective on mistakes by reframing them as valuable learning opportunities. Instead of dwelling on the negative aspects, consider what insights you can glean from the experience. Reflect on how you can grow and improve as a result of the mistake.

PTSD SYMPTOM MANAGEMENT PROGRAM

In this interactive exercise, we'll be using a structured approach developed by Stephanie D. Nelson, a behavioral science officer from the United States Army (Nash, 2019). It's designed to help you work through the symptoms of PTSD. Let's walk through the four stages together:

1. **Addressing Your Trauma**—Developing a Trauma Narrative is the first step toward addressing your past experiences. This process entails writing about your traumatic events in a structured and organized manner.

2. **Experiencing Your Trauma**—This step requires you to actively engage with the memories of your trauma through guided imagery exercises. You'll be encouraged to vividly imagine the details of the traumatic event, allowing yourself to experience the emotions and sensations associated with it. This process can be challenging and emotionally intense, but it's an essential part of the healing journey. By confronting your trauma in a safe and controlled environment, you can begin to process and make sense of your experiences, paving the way for healing and recovery.

3. **Embracing Growth**—We'll then focus on post-traumatic growth (PTG) through three steps:

   i. Embracing freedom of choice—Explore the idea that despite the trauma you've experienced, you still have the power to make choices and shape your life.

ii. Discovering meaning in your trauma—Find meaning and purpose in your traumatic experiences. This is to help you identify lessons learned and valuable insights gained.

iii. Embodying the hero archetype—See yourself as a hero on your healing journey, recognizing your resilience and strength in overcoming adversity.

4. **Organizing Your Memories**—Lastly, organize your traumatic memories using the "mind as a filing cabinet" metaphor. This helps restructure your memories into a more manageable form.

Letter to Past Self

Dear Past Self,

As I reflect on our journey, I want to take a moment to acknowledge the ___________________ (insert challenges) you've faced and the hurdles you've overcome. You've weathered storms that seemed insurmountable at the time, yet here we are, still standing strong.

I want you to know that it was okay to feel ___________________ back then. The struggles, the doubts, the pain—they were all valid experiences that have shaped us into who we are today. You may have felt lost or uncertain at times, but each step you took, no matter how small, led us closer to where we are now.

I wish I could tell you that the road ahead will be smooth and easy, but that wouldn't be true. There will be more challenges, more heartaches, and moments when you'll question everything. But remember, you are resilient. You have a strength within you that you may not fully realize yet.

So, dear Past Self, be gentle with yourself. Forgive yourself for the mistakes you've made and the times you've stumbled. Embrace your flaws and imperfections, for they are what make you beautifully human.

Above all, hold onto hope. Believe in the possibility of a brighter tomorrow, even when the darkness seems overwhelming. Trust that you are capable of overcoming whatever lies ahead, armed with the lessons of the past and the courage to face the future.

With love and compassion,

[Your Name]

As we move forward, "Chapter 3: Embracing Yourself as Part of Healing" builds upon this foundation, guiding you on a path of self-acceptance and empowerment. We'll explore how embracing yourself, flaws and all, is integral to the healing process. From cultivating self-love to nurturing a positive self-image, this chapter will equip you with the tools to embark on a journey of profound transformation.

EMBRACING YOURSELF AS PART OF HEALING

A couple of months ago, my friend opened up to me about their struggles with toxic behavior. They shared how their low self-esteem and stress were causing them to act in harmful ways, especially in relationships. They often felt guilty about their behavior, believing they didn't deserve to be treated with kindness and respect.

As my friend spoke, it became clear how their toxic patterns were driven by their insecurities and negative thoughts about themselves. They constantly doubted their worth, which led them to push people away or sabotage their relationships. Despite wanting to change, they felt stuck in a cycle of self-destructive behavior.

Listening to my friend's story was a wake-up call for both of us. It made me realize how common these struggles are and how important it is to address them with compassion and understanding. My friend's journey taught me that healing begins with acknowledging our vulnerabilities and being willing to seek support and guidance.

Through their experience, I learned that toxic behavior often stems from deep-rooted issues like low self-esteem and stress. It's a reminder that we all deserve love and acceptance, even when we're struggling. By showing empathy toward ourselves and others, we can break free from toxic patterns and create healthier, more fulfilling relationships.

In this chapter, we will explore the transformative journey of self-acceptance and self-care, offering practical insights and strategies to help you navigate through the complexities of embracing yourself as part of healing.

HOW BEING MENTALLY AND EMOTIONALLY HEALTHY HELPS YOU OVERCOME TOXIC BEHAVIORS

Mental and emotional health are fundamental aspects of our journey to overcome toxic behaviors. They form the backbone of our ability to navigate life's challenges and make positive choices.

When our mental and emotional health is compromised, toxic behaviors often emerge. It's like trying to drive a classic car that hasn't been properly maintained—you might encounter rust, mechanical issues, and breakdowns along the way. By prioritizing our mental and emotional well-being, we're essentially restoring the car to its original glory, ensuring it runs smoothly and retains its value.

Being mentally and emotionally healthy is crucial for overcoming toxic behaviors because it provides us with the foundation and resilience needed to confront and change harmful patterns.

Just like restoring a classic car requires meticulous care and maintenance, nurturing our mental and emotional health allows us to address the underlying issues that lead to toxic behaviors. This clarity of thought helps us understand the root causes of our actions and identify healthier alternatives.

HEALTHY HABITS FOR SELF-LOVE

Many of us struggle with self-love for various reasons. It could stem from past experiences, such as childhood trauma or negative feedback from peers or authority figures. Additionally, societal standards and comparisons to others can fuel feelings of inadequacy and self-doubt. For example, if we constantly compare ourselves to the curated lives we see on social media, we may feel like we don't measure up.

How Common Is It to Struggle with Self-Love?

Struggling with self-love is more common than you might think. In today's fast-paced and highly critical society, many people grapple with feelings of unworthiness and self-criticism. Research suggests that a significant portion of the population experiences low self-esteem at some point in their lives. It's essential to remember that you're not alone in this struggle.

Why Is Hating Yourself So Harmful?

Hating yourself can have detrimental effects on your mental, emotional, and physical well-being. Constant self-criticism and negative self-talk can lead to increased stress, anxiety, and depression. It can also impact your relationships and your overall quality of life. For example, if you don't believe in your worth, you may settle for less in relationships or shy away from pursuing your goals and dreams.

Healthy Habits for Self-Love

By practicing the following strategies consistently, you can gradually cultivate a greater sense of self-love and acceptance. Remember, it's a journey, and progress may take time, but you deserve to love and care for yourself.

Practice Self-Care (Even When You Don't Want To)

Self-care means taking care of yourself in different ways, like eating healthy foods, getting enough sleep, exercising, and doing things you enjoy. Even if you don't feel like it, try to do something nice for yourself every day. It could be as simple as taking a relaxing bath or going for a walk in nature.

Robin Sharma, in his book *The 5:00 a.m. Club,* teaches us that the time you least feel like doing something is the best time to do it (Sharma & Alkesh Patel, 2019).

Embrace Imperfections and Mistakes

Nobody is perfect, and it's okay to make mistakes or have flaws. Embrace your imperfections as part of what makes you unique and human. Learn from your mistakes and use them as opportunities for growth and self-improvement.

Instead of berating yourself for falling into a pattern of passive-aggressive behavior or criticizing others, recognize it as an opportunity for growth. For instance, if you catch yourself making a sarcastic remark to a colleague, instead of dwelling on it, reflect on why you reacted that way. Ask yourself what triggered the behavior and how you can respond differently in the future.

Surround Yourself with Supportive People

Having supportive friends and family members can make a big difference in how you feel about yourself. Surround yourself with people who uplift and encourage you and who accept you for who you are. Limit time with those who bring you down or make you feel bad about yourself.

Spend time with friends who make you feel good about yourself and who support your goals and aspirations. Their positivity and encouragement can boost your self-esteem and help you see yourself in a more positive light.

HEALTHY HABITS FOR STRESS MANAGEMENT

Stress can indeed contribute to the manifestation of toxic behaviors. When we experience high levels of stress, we may resort to maladaptive coping mechanisms to alleviate or manage our distress. These coping strategies, although initially aimed at reducing stress, can often result in behaviors that are harmful to us or others.

Toxic behavior can serve as a coping mechanism in times of stress, providing us with a temporary sense of relief or control over our circumstances. For example, imagine a scenario where an individual is under immense pressure to meet a tight deadline at work. Despite their best efforts, they find themselves struggling to keep up with the workload, leading to increased stress and anxiety. To alleviate their distress, they begin to lash out at their coworkers, criticizing their performance and assigning blame for any setbacks.

Instead of seeking constructive solutions or support from their colleagues, this individual resorts to toxic behavior as a means of venting their frustration and regaining a sense of control. However, this behavior only serves to escalate tensions in the workplace and strain interpersonal relationships, ultimately exacerbating their stress levels.

Now, if we are going to stop stress from controlling our reactions to life, we must learn how to manage it effectively.

Identify Stress

Understanding the cause of stress is essential for effectively managing it. Stress can stem from various sources, such as work deadlines, financial pressures, relationship issues, or health concerns. By pinpointing the specific stressors in your life, you can address them more effectively. For instance, if you're stressed about an upcoming presentation at work, acknowledging this allows you to take steps to prepare and alleviate some of that stress.

Recognizing how you feel physically and emotionally when stressed is also crucial. Physically, stress can manifest as muscle tension, headaches, fatigue, or even digestive problems. Emotionally, you may experience anxiety, irritability, sadness, or a sense of overwhelm. Being attuned to these physical and emotional cues helps you identify when stress is affecting you and prompts you to take action to manage it. For example, if you notice yourself feeling tense and anxious before a social event, you can employ relaxation techniques to ease your physical and emotional discomfort.

Furthermore, understanding your reaction to stressors provides insight into your coping mechanisms. Some people may respond to stress by avoiding the source of their anxiety, while others may become hyper-focused on resolving it. For instance, if faced with a looming deadline, one person may procrastinate and distract themselves, while another may work tirelessly to meet the deadline, neglecting self-care in the process. Recognizing your typical responses to stress allows you to evaluate their effectiveness and make adjustments as needed.

Relaxation Techniques

In times of stress, it's important to have effective strategies for relaxation to help alleviate tension and promote a sense of calm. Relaxation techniques offer valuable tools for managing stress and fostering overall well-being. These techniques can be simple yet powerful, providing a way to unwind and recharge amidst life's challenges.

Laugh More

Laughter is a powerful stress reliever that can instantly lighten your mood and reduce tension. When you laugh, your body releases endorphins, which are natural feel-good chemicals that promote relaxation. You can incorporate laughter into your life by watching funny movies or TV shows, spending time with friends who make you laugh, or engaging in activities that bring you joy and amusement.

Massage

Massage therapy involves manipulating the muscles and soft tissues of the body to promote relaxation and alleviate tension. Massage can help reduce stress by lowering levels of cortisol, the stress hormone, and increasing levels of serotonin and dopamine, which are neurotransmitters associated with relaxation and happiness. Whether you opt for a professional massage or practice self-massage techniques at home, incorporating massage into your routine can be an effective way to relieve stress and promote overall well-being.

Deep-Breathing Exercise

Deep-breathing exercises, also known as diaphragmatic breathing or belly breathing, involve taking slow, deep breaths to activate the body's relaxation response. Deep breathing can help reduce stress by calming the nervous system and lowering blood pressure and heart rate. To practice deep-breathing exercises, find a quiet, comfortable space; inhale deeply through your nose, allowing your abdomen to expand; hold your breath for a few seconds; and then exhale slowly through your mouth, allowing your abdomen to contract. Repeat this process several times to promote relaxation and reduce stress.

Physical Techniques

Physical techniques for stress management involve incorporating lifestyle changes and habits that promote physical well-being, which in turn can help alleviate stress and improve overall health.

Be Physically Active

Regular physical activity is one of the most effective ways to reduce stress and promote emotional well-being. Exercise helps release endorphins, those feel-good chemicals that I mentioned earlier, which can act as natural painkillers and mood elevators, leading to feelings of relaxation and happiness. Whether it's going for a brisk walk, practicing yoga, or engaging in strength training, finding enjoyable ways to stay active can significantly reduce stress levels and improve overall health.

Improve Your Sleep Habits

Quality sleep is essential for managing stress and promoting overall health and vitality. Lack of sleep can exacerbate stress levels and impair cognitive function, mood regulation, and immune function. Establishing a regular sleep schedule, creating a relaxing bedtime routine, and optimizing your sleep environment can help improve sleep quality. Prioritizing restful sleep allows your body and mind to rejuvenate, enhancing resilience to stress and supporting emotional well-being.

Stop Using Substances

While substances such as alcohol, nicotine, and drugs may provide temporary relief from stress, they can ultimately worsen stress levels and contribute to long-term health problems. Substance use can interfere with sleep, impair judgment, and exacerbate feelings of anxiety and depression. By avoiding or limiting the use of substances, individuals can better manage stress and protect their physical and mental health. Seeking healthier coping strategies, such as exercise, mindfulness, and social support, can provide more sustainable ways to manage stress and promote well-being.

Cognitive Techniques

Cognitive techniques involve strategies that target thought patterns and beliefs to promote stress reduction and emotional well-being. By adopting cognitive strategies, you can reframe your perceptions of stressors and develop healthier coping mechanisms.

Keep a Journal

Writing down thoughts and feelings in a journal can be a therapeutic way to process emotions and gain insight into stress triggers. Journaling allows individuals to express themselves freely, identify recurring patterns or stressors, and explore potential solutions to problems. By documenting thoughts and emotions, individuals can gain clarity and perspective, leading to greater self-awareness and stress reduction.

Make "Me Time"

Carving out dedicated time for self-care and relaxation is crucial for managing stress and nurturing emotional well-being. "Me time" isn't just about indulging in activities that bring joy and relaxation; it's about learning to appreciate and enjoy spending time alone with yourself. It's an opportunity to tune in to your thoughts, reflect on your day, and explore your inner world. When you embrace solitude, you can cultivate a deeper understanding of yourself and identify areas for personal growth. Prioritizing self-care allows you to recharge mentally and emotionally, fostering a sense of balance and resilience in the face of life's challenges.

HAVING PATIENCE AND LETTING GO OF CONTROL

Meet Matt, a longtime friend who always seemed to be under a cloud of stress. Matt was the type of person who felt the weight of the world on his shoulders, constantly worrying about things he couldn't control.

Every time something didn't go according to plan, Matt would become visibly upset. He'd lash out in frustration or retreat into himself, unable to cope with the unexpected twists and turns of life. His relationships suffered as a result; friends and family found it difficult to connect with him when he was so consumed by worry and anxiety.

Matt's health took a hit, too. The constant stress and tension left him feeling exhausted and drained both mentally and physically. He struggled to find joy in the present moment, always preoccupied with what might go wrong next.

Over time, it became clear that Matt's need for control was holding him back. His inability to let go of the things he couldn't change was causing him unnecessary suffering and preventing him from living life to the fullest.

But then, something shifted for Matt. He began to realize that trying to control every aspect of his life was a losing battle. He started to let go of his need for control and embrace the concept of patience.

As Matt learned to accept the things he couldn't change, he found a newfound sense of peace and contentment. He became less reactive to life's curveballs, responding with grace and composure instead of frustration and anger.

His relationships improved as a result. By letting go of control, Matt was able to foster deeper connections with others, built on trust, empathy, and understanding. He became more present in his interactions, no longer weighed down by worries about the future or regrets about the past.

Not only did Matt's mental and emotional well-being improve, but his physical health also benefited from his newfound mindset. With less stress and tension weighing him down, he felt lighter, more energized, and more resilient in the face of challenges.

Ways to Cultivate Patience in Your Life

Look for small opportunities to practice patience. Start by identifying small moments in your daily routine where you can exercise patience. This could be waiting in line at the grocery store, dealing with traffic, or waiting for a friend to respond to a message. Use these moments as opportunities to practice patience and tolerance.

Shift your perspective. Instead of focusing on immediate gratification or instant results, adopt a long-term perspective. Recognize that some things take time to unfold or achieve, and practice patience by trusting in the process and allowing things to unfold naturally.

Accept what's out of your control. Acceptance is key to cultivating patience. Understand that certain things in life are beyond your control, and instead of resisting or trying to force outcomes, practice acceptance and surrender. Focus on controlling your reactions and responses to situations rather than trying to control external circumstances.

CULTIVATING EMOTIONAL RESILIENCE

Emotional resilience is the ability to bounce back from difficult or stressful situations. It means being able to adapt and cope with challenges, setbacks, and adversities in life without feeling overwhelmed or defeated. Emotional resilience doesn't mean that you won't experience distress or hardship but rather that you have the strength and flexibility to navigate through tough times and emerge stronger.

Developing Emotional Resiliency

Acknowledgment and acceptance—Face reality and sit with your emotions. Feel them for what they are and understand where they come from. This isn't about wallowing; it's about recognizing and accepting your feelings without judgment.

Control what you actually can—You can't eliminate stress or avoid life's challenges, but you can control your reactions to them. Take responsibility for your choices and prepare yourself for life's punches. Prioritize self-care by maintaining physical fitness, consuming a healthy diet, and getting enough sleep. By taking care of yourself, you're creating the physical toughness needed to combat stress.

Find a purpose—Change doesn't happen overnight, and you can't simply will yourself to be happy. You need a deeper reason for wanting to change—a purpose that drives you forward. Whether it's your relationships, your career, or the legacy you want to leave behind, find your purpose and let it guide you. Write it down, refer to it daily, and let it fuel your journey toward emotional resilience.

CONSISTENCY WITH STRIVING TO BE BETTER

In the journey of overcoming my toxic behavior, I've come to realize that the real challenge lies not just in striving to be better but in maintaining consistency in that pursuit. It's easy to muster the motivation to make positive changes and strive for improvement in the beginning, but staying committed to those changes over the long term requires a different level of dedication and perseverance.

Consistency is crucial because it's what ultimately leads to lasting transformation. It's about showing up every day, even when the initial excitement fades and the road ahead seems daunting. Consistency means making a conscious effort to align your actions with your values and goals, even when faced with obstacles and setbacks.

One of the key reasons why consistency is so important is that change doesn't happen overnight. It's a gradual process that requires sustained effort and practice. By consistently taking small steps toward self-improvement, you gradually build momentum and create lasting habits that contribute to your growth and development.

Moreover, consistency builds trust and credibility with yourself. When you consistently follow through on your commitments and stick to your goals, you develop a sense of self-trust and confidence in your ability to overcome challenges and achieve success. This, in turn, reinforces your motivation and resilience, making it easier to stay on course even when faced with adversity.

EMOTIONAL RESILIENCE SELF-ASSESSMENT

Take a moment to reflect on your emotional resilience with the following questions:

1. How do you typically respond to challenges and setbacks?
2. What coping strategies do you rely on during stressful times?
3. Do you tend to bounce back quickly from adversity, or do you find it difficult to recover?
4. How do you nurture your emotional well-being on a regular basis?
5. Are there areas of your life where you feel particularly resilient and areas where you struggle?
6. How do you handle strong emotions like anger, sadness, or anxiety?
7. Do you have a support system in place to help you during tough times?

8. Are there any patterns or habits that you recognize as hindering your emotional resilience?

9. What steps can you take to strengthen your resilience and better cope with life's challenges?

10. How do you prioritize self-care and emotional health in your daily life?

Take your time to answer these questions honestly and reflect on ways you can enhance your emotional resilience.

In this chapter, you've explored the crucial journey of self-acceptance and self-care as essential steps toward healing. By relinquishing the need for control and embracing these principles, you've gained valuable strategies for overcoming toxic behaviors. Through self-compassion and mindfulness, you've cultivated emotional resilience and a more positive outlook on life. Now, as we move into *Chapter 4, Overcoming "Toxic" Behaviors*, you'll dive deeper into addressing specific toxic tendencies and implementing practical tools for lasting change. These strategies will equip you with the patience needed to confront and overcome your most challenging behaviors head-on.

As Chelsea sat across from me at our usual café, sipping her coffee with a furrowed brow, I could sense something was weighing heavily on her mind. After some prodding, she finally opened up about the challenges she was facing in her relationships and personal life.

"I've been doing a lot of reflecting lately," she began, her voice laced with uncertainty. "I've come to realize that I have some really controlling tendencies. Like, I always have to have things my way, you know? I remember last week, during our group project, I kept insisting on my ideas and shutting down others. I even manipulated the situation by making it seem like my way was the only way. It created so much tension, and now I see how it's affected my friendships."

Her admission hung heavy in the air as she continued, "And then there's my relationship with my partner. I catch myself second-guessing their choices all the time, trying to steer things in a direction that suits me better. It's like I'm constantly manipulating the situation to make myself feel more secure, but it's pushing us further apart."

Chelsea's story hit close to home, and I could see the struggle reflected in the eyes of so many others who grapple with similar issues. It's a tough pill to swallow, acknowledging our own toxic behaviors, but it's the first step toward growth and healing.

In this chapter, we'll dive deep into some of the most common toxic behaviors and explore practical strategies for overcoming them. It's not going to be easy, and it'll require some serious self-reflection and hard work. But if Chelsea can find the courage to confront her toxic tendencies, then so can you.

CONSTANT NEGATIVITY

Let's be honest—constant negativity stinks. It's like being stuck in a perpetual rainstorm of complaints, criticisms, and pessimism. Imagine being around someone who always sees the glass as half-empty, who can find fault in even the most beautiful of sunsets. It's draining, demoralizing, and downright exhausting.

Picture this—you're trying to share some good news with your friend, but before you can even finish your sentence, they jump in with a laundry list of everything that could go wrong. Or maybe you're at work, trying to brainstorm ideas for a new project, but every suggestion you make gets shot down with a barrage of negativity.

Now, let's be real about why this is such a problem. Constant negativity not only dampers everyone's mood but also sabotages relationships, kills creativity, and stifles personal growth. When you're constantly focusing on the negative, you're missing out on opportunities for joy, connection, and success.

But here's the kicker—you have the power to change this. It starts with acknowledging that your negativity is holding you back and committing to make a change. Instead of defaulting to criticism and complaints, try focusing on gratitude and positivity. Challenge yourself to find something to be thankful for, even in the midst of challenges. Shift your mindset from one of scarcity to one of abundance.

Here is a simple routine that we can leverage to let go of this constant negativity:

Gratitude Journaling—Every morning or evening, take a few minutes to write down three things you're grateful for. They can be big or small, significant or seemingly insignificant. The act of focusing on gratitude shifts your perspective from what's wrong to what's right in your life. It's a simple yet powerful way to train your brain to notice the positive aspects of your day.

Positive Affirmations—Start each day with a mantra or affirmation that counteracts your default negative thoughts. Choose a phrase that resonates with you, such as, "I am capable and deserving of happiness," or, "I attract positivity into my life." Repeat this affirmation to yourself throughout the day, especially when you catch yourself slipping into negative thinking patterns. Over time, these positive affirmations will become ingrained in your mindset, helping to reshape your outlook on life.

Limiting Negative Input—Take stock of the media, conversations, and environments that contribute to your negativity. Are there certain social media accounts, news outlets, or people in your life that consistently bring you down? Make a conscious effort to limit your exposure to these sources of negativity. Instead, seek out uplifting content, surround yourself with positive influences, and engage in activities that bring you joy and fulfillment.

SELF-CENTEREDNESS

Self-centeredness is wearing blinders in a crowded room—you're only focused on yourself, oblivious to the needs and experiences of those around you. It's constantly talking about yourself without listening to others, prioritizing your own needs and desires above all else, and expecting everyone to cater to your whims.

Imagine you're at a dinner party with friends. As the conversation flows, one person dominates the discussion, constantly steering it back to themselves. They talk about their recent promotion at work, their extravagant vacation plans, and their latest achievements, barely pausing to let others speak.

You notice how they interrupt and talk over others, dismissing their experiences and opinions as unimportant.

It feels like they're competing for attention, craving validation and approval from the group.

Now, put yourself in the shoes of that person's friends and loved ones. You might feel neglected and unimportant like you're just props in their self-centered narrative. It breeds resentment and frustration, eroding trust and intimacy in their relationships.

But it's not just about the impact on others; self-centeredness also stunts your own personal growth and fulfillment. When you're solely focused on yourself, you miss out on the richness and depth that come from connecting with others and understanding their perspectives. You become trapped in a cycle of self-absorption, unable to break free and experience the joy of genuine connection and empathy.

To overcome self-centeredness, you need to start by acknowledging the harmful impact it has on your relationships and personal well-being. Recognize that the world doesn't revolve around you and that true happiness comes from building meaningful connections and contributing to the lives of others.

These simple yet effective strategies will guide you into letting go of this negative trait:

Practice active listening. Instead of dominating conversations, make a conscious effort to listen actively to others. This means truly focusing on what they're saying without interrupting or formulating your response in your head. Practice paraphrasing what they've said to ensure you understand their perspective before sharing your own.

Show empathy. Put yourself in others' shoes and try to understand their feelings and experiences. Ask open-ended questions to encourage them to share more about themselves and validate their emotions without dismissing or minimizing them. Express empathy through both your words and actions to demonstrate that you care about their well-being.

Practice generosity. Cultivate a mindset of generosity by looking for opportunities to support and uplift others. Offer your time, resources, or assistance whenever possible without expecting anything in return. By focusing on the needs and happiness of others, you'll naturally shift away from self-centered tendencies and toward a more compassionate outlook.

BEING CRITICAL

Imagine a scenario where you're at a gathering with friends and one of them excitedly shares an idea they've been working on. Instead of offering encouragement or constructive feedback, you immediately criticize their idea, pointing out flaws and shortcomings without considering their perspective. Your critical remarks deflate their enthusiasm and leave them feeling disheartened and embarrassed in front of the group.

Being critical often involves nitpicking, fault-finding, and focusing on the negatives rather than the positives. It can manifest in various aspects of life, from criticizing others' ideas and actions to being overly self-critical and judgmental.

This behavior is harmful and detrimental because it creates an atmosphere of negativity and discouragement. Constant criticism erodes trust and damages relationships, leading to resentment and alienation. It stifles creativity and innovation, discouraging people from taking risks or sharing their ideas for fear of being criticized.

Being critical often sneaks up on us without us even realizing it. We might believe we're offering helpful solutions or constructive feedback, but in reality, our criticism can be damaging and hurtful. It's essential to recognize the fine line between offering valuable input and being overly critical.

Offer constructive feedback. When providing feedback or expressing concerns, focus on offering constructive suggestions for improvement rather than simply pointing out flaws or shortcomings. Use specific examples and provide actionable steps or recommendations for how they can address the issues. Aim to be supportive and encouraging, emphasizing growth and development rather than criticism and fault-finding.

Find something positive. Make a conscious effort to find something positive or commendable about the situation, idea, or person before voicing any criticism. This could involve acknowledging their effort, creativity, or good intentions. By starting with a positive comment, you set a more constructive tone for the conversation and show appreciation for their efforts.

The suggested changes are necessary because they promote a more positive and supportive environment where people feel valued and encouraged to express themselves freely. By practicing empathy, kindness, and constructive feedback, we can cultivate a culture of collaboration and growth.

TOXIC MANIPULATION

Toxic manipulation is like trying to play a game where you make up the rules as you go along and change them whenever it suits you. You might twist the truth, guilt-trip others, or use emotional blackmail to get your way. It's trying to drive a car with square wheels—sure, you might get somewhere, but you're leaving a trail of damage in your wake.

Imagine you're planning a weekend getaway with friends, but you want to go to a different destination than everyone else. Instead of discussing it openly and finding a compromise, you start dropping subtle hints about how much you've always wanted to visit your preferred spot. You might even manipulate the situation by exaggerating the downsides of the other destinations or making promises you know you won't keep.

But here's the thing—toxic manipulation isn't just a harmless game. It's playing with fire. It erodes trust, damages relationships, and leaves everyone feeling burnt out and exhausted. Plus, it's exhausting for you too!

Constantly trying to manipulate others takes a toll on your mental and emotional well-being, leaving you feeling isolated and unfulfilled.

So, let's cut the charade and ditch the manipulation playbook. Instead, let's focus on building genuine connections and fostering healthy communication through these few actionable steps. It might take some practice, but it's worth it in the end. After all, wouldn't you rather be known for your honesty and integrity than your ability to pull strings behind the scenes?

Practice transparency. Make a conscious effort to be open and honest in your interactions with others. Instead of resorting to manipulation tactics, express your thoughts, feelings, and needs directly. Practice transparency by communicating openly, even when it feels uncomfortable. For example, if you're feeling overwhelmed with work and need assistance, instead of manipulating a colleague into taking on your tasks without their consent, openly communicate your workload and ask for their help.

Respect boundaries. Recognize and respect the boundaries of others. Avoid crossing boundaries or manipulating situations to get your way. Instead, focus on building trust and fostering healthy relationships by honoring the boundaries set by others. Suppose a friend shares a personal story with you in confidence. Rather than using that information to manipulate them or gain leverage in a situation, respect their boundary by keeping the information confidential and refrain from exploiting it for your benefit.

Empower others. Instead of manipulating situations to serve your own interests, empower others to make their own choices and decisions. Encourage autonomy and respect the agency of those around you. By supporting others in making empowered choices, you cultivate trust and mutual respect in your relationships. Let's say you're working on a group project, and you notice a team member struggling with a task. Instead of manipulating the situation to make yourself look better by taking over the task, empower your teammates by offering guidance and support to help them succeed independently.

AVOIDANT TENDENCIES

Avoidant tendencies involve avoiding confrontation, difficult conversations, or responsibilities, often out of fear or discomfort. For example, if you constantly procrastinate on important tasks or dodge discussions about your feelings in relationships, you may exhibit avoidant tendencies.

This behavior can be harmful, as it prevents you from addressing issues head-on, leading to unresolved conflicts, missed opportunities for growth, and strained relationships. Instead of facing challenges directly, you may resort to temporary avoidance tactics that only exacerbate the problem in the long run.

Meet Martin. He was in a relationship with Jade for a couple of years. Everything seemed fine on the surface, but there was a problem lurking beneath the smiles and laughter.

Martin tended to avoid difficult conversations with Jade. Whenever there was a disagreement or tension brewing, he would rather sweep it under the rug than address it head-on. This behavior had become a pattern in their relationship, leaving Jade feeling frustrated and unheard.

For example, one evening, Jade brought up the topic of their future together. She wanted to discuss their long-term goals and aspirations, but Martin quickly changed the subject, deflecting with jokes or excuses. He felt uncomfortable delving into such serious topics and would rather avoid the conversation altogether.

Over time, Jade began to feel disconnected from Martin. She craved open and honest communication, but Martin's avoidant tendencies made it challenging to bridge the gap between them. The unresolved issues piled up, creating tension and resentment in their relationship.

Despite Jade's attempts to initiate discussions and address their issues, Martin continued to dodge the uncomfortable conversations, hoping they'd magically disappear on their own. However, the strain on their relationship only grew as Martin's avoidance drove a wedge between them.

In the end, Martin's avoidant tendencies sabotaged his relationship with Jade, leaving them both feeling unsatisfied and unfulfilled. It was clear that avoiding difficult conversations only led to further disconnection and heartache.

Now, you may be relating to this and wondering how you can help yourself to be a better partner than Martin was with Jade. Here is how:

Set aside dedicated time for communication. Schedule regular check-ins with your partner or loved ones to discuss any concerns, feelings, or issues that may arise. This could be a weekly meeting or a daily check-in where you both have the opportunity to express yourselves openly and honestly.

Focus on listening and not simply hearing. When engaging in conversations, focus on truly understanding the other person's perspective instead of formulating your response. Practice active listening by maintaining eye contact, nodding, and paraphrasing what the other person has said to ensure you're on the same page. This helps foster better communication and prevents misunderstandings.

Recognize avoidance behaviors. Recognize when you're avoiding difficult conversations or situations and challenge yourself to confront them head-on. Instead of retreating or shutting down, take a deep breath and commit to addressing the issue directly. Remind yourself that avoidance only prolongs the problem and creates further tension in your relationships.

LACK OF RESPECT FOR OTHER PEOPLE'S BOUNDARIES

The majority of us struggle with this toxic behavior, trampling over other people's boundaries like we're crossing a field of daisies without a care in the world. Picture this—

you're at a party, and your friend tells you she's not comfortable with you sharing photos of her without her permission. But what do you do? You go ahead and post that embarrassing snapshot of her anyway, thinking it's all in good fun. Meanwhile, she feels betrayed and disrespected, wondering if she can trust you with anything ever again.

Lack of respect for other people's boundaries isn't just a harmless oversight; it's a wrecking ball crashing through the walls of trust and mutual respect in our relationships. It's akin to playing a game of emotional Jenga, except instead of wooden blocks, you're pulling out chunks of trust and understanding until the whole thing comes crashing down.

It's remarkably easy for people to cross boundaries because, well, boundaries aren't always clearly defined. Imagine driving on a road with no lane markings or traffic signs— you'd likely end up drifting into other lanes or missing turns without even realizing it. Similarly, in our interactions with others, boundaries can be vague or unspoken, making it easy to overstep them without intending to.

Moreover, societal norms and cultural expectations often blur the lines of what's acceptable and what's not. We're bombarded with messages that promote a "me first" mentality or encourage us to prioritize our desires above all else. This can lead to a mindset where respecting others' boundaries takes a back seat to fulfilling our own needs or desires.

It's worth noting that personal experiences and upbringing play a significant role in how we perceive and respect boundaries. If someone grew up in an environment where boundaries were routinely ignored or violated, they may struggle to establish healthy boundaries in their own relationships.

When we couple these factors with our inherent tendency to tread over boundaries, it becomes almost inevitable to disregard others' boundaries. However, this should never be an excuse to impose our behaviors on other people.

Here are some actionable steps to overcome this:

Ask for consent. Before assuming or acting on something, ask for consent from the other person. It involves actively seeking permission before engaging in any action or conversation that could potentially infringe on someone else's boundaries. For example, before initiating physical contact, such as a hug or handshake, it's important to ask the other person if they are comfortable with it. Similarly, when discussing personal matters or sensitive topics, asking for consent signals respect for the other person's emotional boundaries and allows them the opportunity to decline or set limits on the conversation.

Set clear boundaries yourself. Lead by example by establishing and communicating your own boundaries clearly and assertively. This could include specifying your preferences regarding personal space, communication frequency, or topics that are off-limits. Assertively communicating your boundaries sends a clear message to others about your expectations and encourages them to reciprocate by respecting your limits. Additionally, setting boundaries helps you maintain a sense of autonomy and self-respect, empowering you to prioritize your own well-being in all interactions.

PASSIVE AGGRESSIVENESS

Picture this—you're at work, and you've asked your colleague to complete a task by the end of the day. Instead of acknowledging your request directly, they respond with a forced smile and a vague, "Sure, I'll see what I can do," while rolling their eyes behind your back. Later, you find out they didn't even attempt to start the task, leaving you scrambling to pick up the pieces.

Now, why is this harmful? Passive-aggressive behavior creates a toxic environment filled with tension, frustration, and mistrust. It undermines clear communication and erodes teamwork, leading to decreased productivity and morale. Plus, it's just plain exhausting to deal with the constant guessing games and hidden agendas.

When we embrace passive-aggressive tendencies, we're essentially sabotaging our own relationships and success. By avoiding direct communication and resorting to underhanded tactics, we're not only hindering our personal growth but also the growth of those around us.

So, how do we kick this toxic habit to the curb?

Practice conflict resolution skills. Learn effective conflict resolution strategies to address conflicts or disagreements constructively. Focus on finding mutually satisfactory solutions rather than escalating conflicts or harboring resentment. Use techniques such as active listening, empathy, and compromise to foster understanding and reach a resolution collaboratively. Passive-aggressive behavior can exacerbate conflicts and undermine relationships, leading to further tension and mistrust. Effective conflict resolution promotes healthier communication patterns and strengthens interpersonal connections, fostering greater harmony and cooperation.

Practice direct communication. Instead of resorting to passive-aggressive remarks or behavior, express your thoughts and feelings directly and assertively. Use "I" statements to communicate your needs and concerns without blaming or criticizing others. Practice active listening skills to understand the perspectives of others and foster open dialogue. Passive-aggressive behavior often stems from underlying feelings of resentment, frustration, or powerlessness. Direct communication promotes honesty, transparency, and mutual respect in relationships, reducing the need for passive-aggressive tactics.

Practice self-reflection. Take time to reflect on your thoughts, feelings, and behaviors, especially in situations where you are prone to passive-aggressive tendencies. Consider the underlying reasons for your passive-aggressive reactions, such as feelings of insecurity, fear of confrontation, or unmet needs. Challenge negative thought patterns and explore healthier ways to express yourself and address conflicts. Self-reflection is a key component of emotional intelligence and self-awareness, allowing you to identify and address underlying issues that contribute to passive-aggressive behavior.

HYPOCRISY

Hypocrisy is wearing a mask that says one thing while your actions scream another. Picture this—Mike, the self-proclaimed eco-warrior, preaches about environmental sustainability while tossing his plastic water bottles into the trash with careless abandon. Or Milly, the advocate for kindness and compassion, spreads gossip behind closed doors faster than wildfire on a windy day. Hypocrisy is the art of saying one thing and doing another, often with a side of self-righteousness and a sprinkle of insincerity.

But why is hypocrisy such a big deal? Well, let me break it down for you. When you preach one thing and practice another, you erode trust faster than a sandcastle in a tsunami. Your words lose their power, your actions lose their integrity, and your credibility takes a nosedive straight into the realm of disbelief. You become that person nobody wants to take seriously, the one who talks the talk but never walks the walk.

And let's not forget the impact of hypocrisy on those around you. Imagine being on the receiving end of someone's hypocritical behavior. It's like a slap in the face with a velvet glove—soft on the outside but oh-so-painful on the inside. You feel betrayed, misled, and downright duped. And if you're unlucky enough to be the target of their hypocrisy, well, let's just say it's a special kind of torture that no one should have to endure.

No one wants to be labeled a hypocrite, and I'm pretty sure you're no exception. The mere thought of being called out for saying one thing and doing another can send shivers down anyone's spine. Imagine being caught with your hand in the cookie jar while preaching the virtues of a sugar-free diet. But here's the thing—acknowledging our own hypocrisy is the first step toward growth and authenticity.

How do I stop being a hypocrite?

Hold yourself accountable. Take responsibility for your actions and their consequences. When you catch yourself acting hypocritically, acknowledge it openly and commit to making amends. Holding yourself accountable fosters personal growth and reinforces integrity in your behavior.

Embrace authenticity. Strive to live authentically by aligning your actions with your true beliefs and values. Be honest with yourself and others about who you are and what you stand for. Authenticity breeds trust and respect, creating meaningful connections with those around you.

Challenge your biases. Examine your beliefs and attitudes to identify any underlying biases that may contribute to hypocrisy. Challenge yourself to confront and address these biases through education, exposure to diverse perspectives, and open-mindedness.

Seek feedback. Actively solicit feedback from trusted friends, family members, or mentors about your behavior and its alignment with your values. Constructive feedback can provide valuable insights and help you identify areas for improvement.

In this chapter, we've laid bare some of the tough truths about overcoming toxic behaviors. We've seen how they hold us back and disrupt our connections with others. But here's the kicker—acknowledging these behaviors and making a conscious choice to overcome them is just the beginning. It's about facing the mirror and recognizing the good, the bad, and the downright ugly within ourselves.

Now, as we move forward, picture yourself armed with newfound awareness and a determination to change. It's not about perfection; it's about progress. The next chapter isn't just another set of instructions; it's a roadmap to personal transformation with daily progress. So, buckle up because we're about to cultivate strategies that'll help you not only survive but thrive.

HELP OTHERS ALONG THE ROAD TO SELF-DISCOVERY

Not until we are lost do we begin to understand ourselves.

HENRY DAVID THOREAU

You are now halfway through your reading journey, and I hope that you have made one of the most powerful realizations there is—you are brave, honest, and committed... so much so that you have taken on an undoubtedly tough challenge: that of knowing yourself. I mentioned in the introduction that what led me to my path to self-discovery was hitting rock bottom in my relationships. When loved ones tell us that our toxicity is hurting them, it is so easy to point the finger and place the blame on them. Yet we gain very little by expecting others to dance to our rhythm. We can only change ourselves, and when a voice inside us tells us that we are gaslighting, trying to control others, or displaying jealous behaviors, the best thing we can do is listen to it.

Emotions like anger and disappointment can be painful, but they are also powerful signals worth listening to. The biggest losses and disappointments are also the greatest opportunities to look within and think about the thoughts, emotions, and behaviors that haven't been doing us or our loved ones justice.

Thus far, you have seen how traumatic experiences and entrenched family patterns can lead to toxic behavioral partners. You have also discovered how strategies such as effective stress management, reframing negativity, and putting an end to the blame game can propel you toward much healthier and happier relationships. If this book is making a difference to your self-esteem and outlook on relationships, then I hope I can ask you to briefly share your thoughts with others.

By leaving a review of this book on Amazon, you'll help other people who wish to work on their toxicity know that there are concrete, effective changes they can make from day one.

Simply by letting them know what resonated most strongly with you and perhaps sharing a bit about your own story, you'll let them know that their self-honesty will take them far.

Thanks for your support. I wish you all the best in your quest to adopt healthy habits that boost your love for others and yourself.

Scan the QR code below:

CHAPTER 5

YOUR DAILY PROGRESS, UNLEASHED

When overcoming toxic behavior, we face a huge challenge—the relentless cycle of inconsistency and frustration. Despite our best intentions, we often struggle to make lasting changes in our behavior. Each day starts with a surge of motivation, but as the day unfolds, it often gets overtaken by habitual behaviors and justifications. It's like taking one step forward and two steps back, leaving us feeling disheartened and stuck.

In the pages ahead, we'll jump into practical strategies and tools to unleash your daily progress. You'll learn how to cultivate consistency, build resilience, and stay committed to your journey of self-improvement.

HOW TO USE SMART GOALS TO OVERCOME TOXIC BEHAVIOR

A SMART goal is akin to having a well-structured strategy for achieving your objectives. It stands for **s**pecific, **m**easurable, **a**chievable, **r**elevant, and **t**ime-bound.

Basically, it's a way to make sure your goals are clear, doable, and have a deadline. Imagine if Batman had a plan for every mission, right down to the gadgets he needs and when he'll finish—that's a SMART goal!

Here's how to use the framework to set healthy behavior goals:

Specific—Be super clear about what you want to achieve. Instead of saying, "I want to be healthier," try, "I want to exercise for 30 minutes, five days a week."

Measurable—Make sure you can track your progress. It's like keeping score in a game. If your goal is to eat more veggies, you could track how many servings you eat each day.

Achievable—Don't try to leap tall buildings in a single bound! Set goals that you know you can reach with a little effort. Starting with a small goal, like walking for 15 minutes a day, is much easier than running a marathon.

Relevant—Your goals should matter to you and fit into your life. It's like choosing the right tool for the job. If your goal is to reduce stress, maybe trying meditation or yoga would be more relevant than learning to juggle chainsaws!

Time-Bound—Give yourself a deadline. This adds a sense of urgency, like having a countdown clock ticking away. Instead of saying, "I'll exercise more someday," say, "I'll run a 5k race in three months."

Here are a few goals we can set to help us overcome toxic behaviors:

- **Compromise**—Find a middle ground or make concessions in conflicts or decisions. For example, agreeing to watch a comedy movie instead of an action will keep everyone happy.
- **Honesty**—Be truthful and sincere in your words and actions. It's about being a beacon of truth, fighting lies and deceit with your unwavering honesty.
- **Fighting Fair**—Resolve conflicts without resorting to insults, blame, or aggression. Imagine resolving conflicts using words instead of fists—no cheap shots allowed!
- **Individuality**—Embrace and celebrate your uniqueness and allow others to do the same.
- **Mutual Respect**—Treat others with dignity, kindness, and consideration. Think of it as adhering to a code of honor—always showing respect to friends, foes, and everyone in between!
- **Good Communication**—Express yourself clearly and listen actively to others. This allows you to understand exactly what someone needs, whether they're saying it aloud or not!

Here is how you set a SMART goal in action:

Specific—"I want to stop manipulating others by using guilt-tripping tactics in my interactions."

Measurable—"I will track instances of guilt-tripping behavior by keeping a journal and noting down each time I catch myself using manipulative tactics."

Achievable—"Reducing guilt-tripping behavior is feasible for me as I recognize it as a harmful pattern in my interactions. I am committed to making changes, and I am willing to put in the effort to improve."

Relevant—"Eliminating guilt trips aligns with my goal of building healthier and more authentic relationships. It will foster trust and mutual respect in my interactions with others."

Time-Bound—"I will significantly reduce guilt-tripping behavior within the next three months by actively monitoring my communication patterns, seeking feedback from trusted individuals, and practicing alternative ways of expressing my needs and emotions."

KNOWING YOUR TRIGGERS

In Chapter 1, we embarked on a journey of self-discovery by exploring the question, "Are you toxic?" We discovered that understanding our toxic traits requires more than just acknowledging their existence; it involves recognizing the situations, emotions, or interactions that trigger them. These triggers can vary from person to person and can stem from past experiences, learned behaviors, or internal conflicts. Triggers are those little landmines that set off a chain reaction of negative emotions and behaviors, often leading us down a path we'd rather not travel.

To unleash daily progress in overcoming toxic behaviors, we must develop a heightened awareness of our triggers. This means paying close attention to our thoughts, feelings, and reactions in different situations. By understanding what sets off our toxic behaviors, we can anticipate challenging scenarios and proactively implement strategies to manage them effectively.

Step back. Imagine you're in a heated argument with a loved one. As tensions rise, you feel the familiar surge of anger and frustration building within you, like a pressure cooker reaching its boiling point. Instead of letting emotions take control, take a step back, both physically and mentally. It's fundamental to press pause on a fiery exchange, allowing for a moment of reflection amidst the emotional turbulence. This simple act provides the distance needed to gain perspective and prevent the situation from escalating further.

Trace the roots. After hitting the pause button, it's time to put on your detective hat. Dive into the murky waters of your emotions and trace back the roots of that trigger. Ask yourself probing questions like, "What exactly set me off?" or, "Why am I feeling this way?" Here, you are unraveling a tangled ball of yarn to find the elusive thread that started it all. When you dig deep into the past events or thoughts that ignited your reaction, you uncover the hidden triggers lurking beneath the surface.

Get curious. Now that you've identified the trigger and traced its roots, it's time to embrace curiosity. Dive into the depths of your understanding and ask yourself, "What can I learn from this trigger?" Explore the nuances of your reactions and the underlying causes. This is your chance to dissect the trigger, examining it from all angles. By adopting a curious mindset, you empower yourself to glean insights that can guide you toward more constructive responses in the future.

Strategies to Learn to Manage Triggers in the Moment

In our journey to overcome toxic behaviors, one of the most powerful tools we can equip ourselves with is the ability to manage triggers in the moment.

Own your feelings. When a trigger arises, acknowledge and own your feelings without judgment. Recognize that it's okay to feel what you're feeling, but it's also crucial to take responsibility for your reactions.

Give yourself some space. In the heat of the moment, give yourself permission to step away if needed. Sometimes, a brief pause can prevent impulsive reactions and allow you to gather your thoughts before responding.

Communicate. Effective communication is key to managing triggers in the moment. Express your feelings and concerns calmly and assertively. Use "I" statements to convey your emotions without blaming others. For instance, instead of "You never listen to me!" say, "I feel unheard when I try to express my thoughts and feelings." Do you see how the focus shifts from blaming the other person to expressing one's own feelings and experiences? Additionally, listening is equally important in effective communication. Just as you want the other person to understand you, it's essential to consider that they also desire for you to understand them. Actively listening to their perspective and taking responsibility for how your words and actions affect them fosters mutual understanding and respect.

Practice Long-Term Healing

While managing triggers in the moment is crucial for immediate relief, long-term healing focuses on addressing underlying issues and building resilience for lasting change. Toxic behaviors often stem from ingrained patterns and habits that have developed over time. Long-term healing allows you to identify these destructive patterns and break free from them.

Identify toxic relationship patterns. Ever find yourself stuck in a cycle of toxic relationships, like a bad rerun of a soap opera? Reflect on past relationships and spot common patterns or red flags. Are you always the one giving while others take? Do you constantly find yourself in drama-filled situations?

Work on mindfulness. Picture this—you're stuck in traffic, boiling with frustration, ready to blow your top. Instead of letting road rage take the wheel, practice mindfulness. Take a deep breath and focus on the present moment. Notice the sensations in your body, the rhythm of your breath, and the sights and sounds around you. By grounding yourself in the here and now, you can diffuse tension and regain control over your reactions.

Keep a mood journal. If we are being honest, life can be a rollercoaster of emotions with highs, lows, and loop-de-loops. To navigate this emotional whirlwind, start keeping a mood journal. Grab a notebook or download a journaling app and jot down your thoughts and feelings each day. Track your moods, triggers, and any patterns you notice. Over time, you'll gain valuable insights into your emotional landscape and learn to recognize warning signs before they escalate.

Talk to a professional. It's time to call in the big guns—no, not the Avengers, but a professional therapist or counselor. Think of them as your emotional Sherpa, guiding you through the treacherous terrain of your psyche. Whether you're dealing with past trauma, anxiety, or toxic behaviors, a therapist can provide invaluable support and guidance. So, don't be shy—schedule that therapy session and start your journey toward healing and growth.

EMBRACE GROWTH AND CHANGE

Look, let's get one thing straight—none of us are perfect. We're all flawed humans stumbling through this crazy journey called life. But here's the kicker—it's less about where we start and more about where we are headed. The real difference lies in our willingness to embrace growth and change and establish room for daily improvement.

Think about it like this—imagine you're a plant (stick with me here). You start off as a tiny seed buried deep in the soil. But with the right conditions—sunlight, water, and a whole lot of tender, loving care—you begin to sprout, reaching for the sky and unfurling your leaves. Sure, you might encounter some obstacles along the way, like pesky pests, droughts, or the occasional rogue lawnmower, but you adapt, you grow, and you thrive.

In the same way, embracing growth and change is about cultivating that inner resilience, that hunger for improvement, no matter what life throws your way. It's about being open to new experiences, stepping out of your comfort zone, and daring to challenge the status quo.

MAINTAINING PROGRESS AND AVOIDING RELAPSE TO THE TOXIC BEHAVIOR

As I crafted this book, I realized the importance of practicality. In my own journey of overcoming challenging patterns, I encountered countless messages urging me to "communicate better," or, "believe in myself." But let's face it, those vague encouragements weren't cutting it. That's why I knew we needed actionable strategies—ones that actually get results. So here are some battle-tested tactics I've discovered for maintaining progress and avoiding relapse into our toxic patterns.

Make a list. Write down all the situations or triggers that tend to push you back into those toxic behaviors. Seeing them on paper can help you understand them better and come up with a game plan to tackle them. For example, let's say one of your triggers is criticism from others. Your game plan could include the following steps:

1. When you encounter criticism, pause and acknowledge that it's triggering for you. Take a moment to understand why it affects you.
2. Reflect on your reaction to criticism. Are you feeling defensive or insecure? Understanding your emotional response can help you address it more effectively.
3. Instead of immediately reacting defensively or lashing out, try to reframe criticism as constructive feedback. Consider the intentions behind the criticism and whether there may be any truth to it.

Remove the cues. Sometimes, it's the little things that trigger us without us even realizing it. Take a good look at your environment and identify any cues or triggers that might be contributing to your toxic behaviors. Then, do your best to eliminate or avoid them. Let's say you're trying to reduce your procrastination habit. You notice that every time you sit down to work at your desk, you end up getting distracted by your smartphone notifications. In this case, the cue to remove would be your smartphone from your immediate workspace. You could designate a specific area for your phone, away from your work area, or use apps or settings that minimize notifications during work hours.

Replace it. You know the saying, "Out with the old, in with the new"? Well, it applies here, too. Instead of falling back into those toxic patterns, find healthier alternatives. If stress leads you to binge-eat junk food, try going for a walk or doing some deep breathing exercises instead. Replace the old habits with ones that serve you better. For example, identify sources of negative self-talk, such as certain social media accounts or self-critical thoughts, and limit your exposure to them. Unfollow accounts that promote unrealistic standards or challenge negative thoughts with positive affirmations. Alternatively, place sticky notes with uplifting messages or affirmations in areas where you're prone to negative self-talk, like your bathroom mirror or workstation. Surround yourself with reminders of your worth and capabilities.

Reward yourself. Celebrate your victories, no matter how small. Treat yourself to something nice when you reach a milestone or make progress toward your goals. Instead of relying on unhealthy indulgences, consider treating yourself to activities or experiences that contribute to your overall well-being. Whether it's a relaxing massage to unwind, a night out enjoying a comedy show, or a fun game night with friends, choose rewards that align with your values and support your journey toward personal growth. These healthy treats not only acknowledge your progress but also nurture your physical, emotional, and social health, ensuring that your rewards contribute to your overall well-being.

Find Lasting Happiness in Your New and Healthier Behavior

The ultimate goal is not just to change your behavior temporarily but to create lasting change that brings you genuine happiness and fulfillment. Keep your eyes on the prize and enjoy the journey of becoming the best version of yourself.

Discover your why. Take some time to reflect on why you want to make these changes in your life. What are your values and aspirations? Understanding your deeper reasons for wanting change can help fuel your motivation. And hey, it won't kill you to write these down on paper or in your notes app.

Set meaningful goals. Instead of focusing solely on outcomes, set goals that align with your values and aspirations. When your goals are meaningful to you, you'll feel more motivated to work toward them. Utilize our section on SMART goals to go about this.

Celebrate progress. Acknowledge and celebrate your progress along the way. Recognize the small victories and milestones you achieve, as they indicate that you're moving in the right direction. This is not a call for a party, but of course, who am I to stop you? I mean, if you can manage to go a month without manipulating anyone, you deserve to celebrate how far you've come. It's within these simple moments that we find happiness and establish lasting change.

Practice gratitude. Cultivate a mindset of gratitude by regularly reflecting on the things you're thankful for in your life. This can help shift your focus from what you lack to what you already have, boosting your overall happiness and motivation. It can be as simple as, "I'm glad I didn't cross my friend's boundaries today."

Find joy in the process. In my personal quest to fulfill my potential, I've come to realize that potential is a journey, not a destination. It's our capacity to evolve continuously into something greater. Once we reach a milestone, new possibilities emerge, beckoning us to strive further. It's akin to the adage, "It's never tomorrow; it's always today." Our potential is ever-shifting, just as we are. We're never truly finished; perfection remains elusive, and we shouldn't delay our happiness until its attainment. The essence lies in the endeavor itself. Some might ask, "Well, then, what's the point in trying?" The point *is* the trying. When we are learning, growing, changing, progressing—whatever you want to call it—we are moving toward our potential. It's the movement that keeps us alive. It's being a little bit better than we were yesterday. It's expanding our potential. We must find happiness in the progress and the expansion.

Embracing this perspective means finding joy in the process of self-improvement. It's about relishing the growth, learning, and development that accompany each step forward. When I first confronted my toxic behaviors, I yearned for immediate transformation. Yet, I soon grasped the reality that altering ingrained habits demands patience and time. I learned to grant myself grace and embrace the journey's intricacies. Through this evolution, I discovered the profound satisfaction of shedding negativity and embracing positivity. It's about cherishing the journey, celebrating each small triumph, and finding contentment in progress. Every stride forward represents an opportunity to unlock fresh potential and embrace a more vibrant, fulfilling existence.

Practice self-compassion. Be kind to yourself and practice self-compassion, especially during setbacks or challenges. Remember that nobody is perfect, and it's okay to have setbacks along the way. Treat yourself with the same kindness and understanding you would offer to a friend facing similar struggles.

TRIGGER TRACKER

This worksheet provides a structured system to help you establish daily progress by incorporating actionable assignments.

Assignment 1: Identify Your Triggers

Take a moment to reflect on the situations, people, or emotions that tend to trigger negative reactions in you. For example, criticism from your boss, crowded spaces, or feeling ignored by loved ones are common triggers. Write down these triggers in the space provided below.

____

____

____

____

Assignment 2: Recognize Your Reactions

Think about how you typically react when faced with these triggers. Describe your reactions honestly and write down the trigger and your reaction in the space provided.

Trigger: Criticism from boss

Reaction: Feelings of defensiveness and anger, followed by shutting down and withdrawing from the conversation

____

____

____

____

____

____

____

____

____

____

Assignment 3: Identify the Root Cause

Now that you've recognized your triggers and reactions, it's time to dig deeper and uncover the root causes behind them. Think about why these triggers elicit such strong responses from you. Consider past experiences, beliefs, or unresolved emotions that may be contributing to your reactions. Write down the root cause of each trigger in the space provided below.

Trigger: When someone criticizes my work

Root cause: Feeling of insecurity stemming from childhood experiences of not feeling good enough

____

____

____

____

____

____

____

____

____

____

____

Assignment 4: Plan Your Response

Consider how you would like to react differently the next time you encounter these triggers. Write down a healthier and more constructive response to each trigger in the space provided.

Trigger: When someone interrupts me while I'm speaking in a meeting

Right reaction next time: Instead of becoming defensive or shutting down, I will calmly assert myself and politely ask for the opportunity to finish speaking

____

____

____

____

____

____

We've been talking about cultivating consistency, building resilience, and staying committed to our journey of self-improvement.

So, how do we do this? It starts with setting SMART goals—those specific, measurable, achievable, relevant, and time-bound targets. We've got to be clear about what we want to achieve, track our progress, and give ourselves a deadline.

But it's not just about setting goals; it's about recognizing our triggers and learning to manage them in the moment. We've got to own our feelings, give ourselves some space when needed, and communicate assertively without blaming others.

And let's not forget about long-term healing. This is where we identify toxic relationship patterns, work on mindfulness, keep a mood journal, and seek professional support when needed. It's about digging deep, tracing the roots of our behaviors, and embracing growth and change with open arms.

But I get it—maintaining being progress and avoiding relapse can feel like trying to navigate a maze blindfolded. That's why we've got to make a list, identify the cause, remove the cues, and replace those toxic behaviors with healthier alternatives. And when we stumble along the way, we've got to give ourselves some grace, celebrate our victories, and keep pushing forward with persistence.

Ultimately, the goal is to create lasting change that brings us genuine happiness and fulfillment. So, let's discover our why, set meaningful goals, celebrate our progress, practice gratitude, find joy in the process, and above all, show ourselves some self-compassion along the way.

In Part III of our book, we immerse ourselves in the realm of nurturing genuine relationships with others. Drawing from the wisdom gained in Parts I and II, we embark on a journey filled with practical insights and actionable strategies. From overcoming manipulative tendencies to fostering constructive dialogues, this section is dedicated to empowering you to forge authentic connections in your life.

PART THREE
BUILDING GENUINE RELATIONSHIPS WITH OTHERS

Personal relationships are the fertile soil from which all advancement, all success, and all achievement in real life grow.

BEN STEIN

Foregoing toxic behaviors requires a multifaceted approach, but perhaps one of the most crucial strategies is building genuine relationships with others. In Part III of the book, we delve into this essential aspect, recognizing the transformative power of authentic human connections. Here, we explore three key themes: conquering your manipulative mindset, nurturing heartfelt ties, and cultivating positive conversations. These themes underscore the importance of fostering meaningful interactions, cultivating empathy, and fostering trust in our relationships.

CHAPTER 6
CONQUER YOUR MANIPULATIVE MINDSET

Anthony was an average guy, or so he thought. He didn't realize it, but his manipulative tendencies slowly chipped away at his relationships. His habit of always needing to be the center of attention ruined important bonds he held with others. At social gatherings, Anthony constantly steered the conversation back to himself, overshadowing others and making them feel invisible. His friends started to notice, but Anthony brushed off their concerns, insisting that he was just naturally charismatic.

Anthony had a knack for playing the victim. Whenever something went wrong, Anthony was quick to blame others and make excuses for his behavior. He never took responsibility for his actions, instead painting himself as the innocent party in every situation. There was this particular evening when Anthony and his friends planned a movie night. As they gathered at Anthony's apartment, ready to unwind and enjoy a few films, things quickly took a turn for the worse.

Anthony had forgotten to rent the movies everyone was excited about. His friends seemed a bit disappointed, but nothing serious—until Anthony, feeling guilty, decided to justify himself with a frustrating tale about how busy and stressed he had been and how his roommate should have reminded him. Now, everyone was annoyed. Forgetting about their plans was one thing, but not taking ownership and going on as if nothing was ever his responsibility was what really ruined the night. Small mistakes are easily forgiven, but acting like the world is out to get you and, as a result, never owning your mistakes kills connection with people. It's dishonest and fake. Take ownership and be real with your friends; they'll respect you and forgive you for your small mistakes.

Then, there was Anthony's tendency to manipulate people into doing what he wanted. Whether it was guilt-tripping his girlfriend into doing his chores or gaslighting her into doubting her own feelings, Anthony always found a way to get his way. He didn't see anything wrong with bending the truth or using emotional manipulation to achieve his goals, but it took a toll on his relationships.

AM I MANIPULATIVE?

Being manipulative means attempting to control or influence others through deceitful or cunning tactics. It often happens when individuals feel insecure, lack confidence, or have a strong desire for power and control over others. Manipulative behavior may also stem from past experiences where manipulation was used to achieve personal goals or meet emotional needs. Jeff, a long-time friend, once confided in me about why he often comes off as manipulative. He shared that in his foster home where he grew up, manipulation was the order of business. Everything was achieved through manipulation, whether it was through physical or emotional means. This environment ingrained the habit of manipulation in him, shaping the way he interacted with others in adulthood.

Sometimes, we do things with good intentions, thinking we're helping others or teaching them a lesson. But even with good intentions, our actions can still be manipulative. We might not even realize it because we believe we're doing the right thing. This can happen when we want to control a situation or push someone to do something because we think it's for their own good. However, this behavior disrespects the freedom and choices of others.

For example, let's say you want your friend to stop smoking because you're worried about their health. So, you start giving them ultimatums or guilt-tripping them whenever they light up a cigarette. You may think you're helping them quit, but you're actually manipulating them into changing their behavior based on your own beliefs and desires, not theirs. This undermines their autonomy and can strain your relationship.

Similarly, imagine you're trying to convince your partner to go on a diet because you want them to be healthier. You might start by subtly criticizing their eating habits or making comments about their weight, all with the intention of nudging them toward your idea of a healthier lifestyle. But in reality, you're manipulating them into conforming to your standards of what is healthy without considering their own preferences or needs.

You'll Go to Great Lengths to Get Your Way

Imagine you're planning a group outing with your friends, but they want to go to a restaurant you don't like. Instead of expressing your preference calmly, you start subtly suggesting other options, highlighting flaws in their choice, or even offering to pay for everyone if they choose your preferred venue. You might even go as far as manipulating the conversation or the group dynamic to steer them toward your choice without directly stating your opinion. In this scenario, you're willing to manipulate the situation to ensure you get your way, even if it means disregarding the preferences of others.

You Have a Hard Time Directly Voicing Your Needs

Picture a situation where you're unhappy with your workload at work, but you're afraid of confronting your boss about it. Instead of having an open conversation, you resort to passive-aggressive behavior, such as repeatedly missing deadlines or making sarcastic remarks about your workload during team meetings. By avoiding direct communication, you're indirectly trying to manipulate your boss into reducing your workload without explicitly expressing your needs. This reluctance to voice your concerns directly can lead to misunderstandings and strained relationships, both professionally and personally.

We Tend to Project onto Others

Sometimes, we feel insecure about our own work performance, but instead of acknowledging it, we start criticizing our colleague's work. We tend to say things like, "You're always making mistakes," or, "You never pull your weight around here," to deflect attention away from your own insecurities. By projecting onto others, you manipulate the situation to avoid facing your own issues.

You Lie

Have you ever been in a situation where you're running late for a social gathering, but instead of being honest about the reason, you make up an elaborate excuse to avoid taking responsibility? You might claim that you got stuck in traffic when, in reality, you overslept or simply lost track of time. By lying about the situation, you manipulate others into believing a false narrative to avoid facing potential consequences or judgment.

You Make People Feel Guilty

Think about a situation where you want a friend to do something for you, but they decline because they have other plans. Instead of accepting their decision gracefully, you start making them feel guilty by saying things like, "I thought you were a true friend," or, "I always help you out when you need it." By playing on their emotions, you manipulate them into feeling obligated to fulfill your request, even if it inconveniences them.

You Don't Keep Promises

Imagine you promised your friend that you would help them move next weekend, but when the time comes, you make excuses and bail out. Maybe you claim to be sick or suddenly have other plans, leaving your friend in a tough spot. When you fail to follow through on your commitment, you manipulate the situation to prioritize your own convenience over their needs.

You Do Nice Things—With Expectations

Consider a scenario where you buy your partner an expensive gift, but deep down, you're secretly expecting something in return—a gesture of appreciation, validation, or even reciprocation in the form of an equally lavish gift. By attaching strings to your acts of kindness, you manipulate the dynamics of the relationship, turning genuine gestures into transactions driven by self-interest.

You Punish People When You Don't Get Your Way

Think about a time when you disagreed with a friend's decision, and instead of respecting their autonomy, you resorted to passive-aggressive behavior or outright hostility to make them reconsider. Maybe you give them the cold shoulder, spread rumors behind their back, or even threaten to end the friendship if they don't comply with your wishes. By using punishment as a means of control, you manipulate others into conforming to your desires, regardless of their own wants or needs.

You're Overly Persuasive

Imagine you're trying to convince your colleague to take on extra work for a project, even though they're already overwhelmed with their current workload. Instead of respecting their boundaries and considering their well-being, you relentlessly pressure them with persuasive arguments, guilt-tripping tactics, or false promises of rewards or recognition.

TYPES OF MANIPULATION (AND HOW TO STOP THEM)

Manipulation, as we've come to understand, manifests in various forms, each with its own set of tactics and strategies aimed at influencing others to act in a desired way. Manipulation is a toxic behavior that can severely impact our relationships with others. To build genuine connections, it's imperative that we recognize our manipulative patterns and work toward overcoming them. By doing so, we can foster healthier and more authentic relationships based on trust, respect, and mutual understanding.

Gaslighting

Gaslighting is a manipulative tactic where one person seeks to distort or undermine another person's perception of reality, causing them to doubt their own thoughts, feelings, and experiences. This form of manipulation can have damaging effects on the victim's mental and emotional well-being, leading to confusion, self-doubt, and a loss of confidence.

For example, Daisy confronts her partner, Henry, about his excessive spending habits. Instead of acknowledging the issue, Henry responds by saying, "You're overreacting. I've barely spent any money lately. You must be imagining things." Over time, Daisy begins to question her perception of the situation, wondering if she's being too critical or unreasonable, even though the evidence of Henry's spending is clear.

Now, some of us play the role of Henry in our daily lives, constantly striving to sow seeds of doubt in others' feelings and decisions to boost our own egos.

By following this structured approach to self-reflection, you can gradually increase your self-awareness, identify gaslighting patterns, and take proactive steps toward healthier relationships and communication.

Set aside dedicated time. Allocate a specific time each day for self-reflection.

Morning Reflection— Start your day by taking a few moments to reflect on instances of gaslighting that may have occurred recently. Consider how these experiences made you feel and how they may have impacted your perception of reality. Use this time to reaffirm your own thoughts and feelings, separate from any attempts at manipulation.

Evening Review— Before bedtime, set aside time to review your interactions throughout the day. Pay particular attention to any moments where you felt invalidated or doubted by someone else's gaslighting tactics. Reflect on how you responded in those situations and whether there are any patterns or triggers to be aware of.

Weekly Evaluation— Dedicate one day each week to conduct a more in-depth evaluation of your experiences with gaslighting. Look back on the past week and identify any recurring patterns or behaviors that may indicate gaslighting attempts. Take note of any instances where you successfully recognized and resisted gaslighting, as well as areas where you may still need to improve.

Monthly Assessment— Once a month, take a step back to assess your overall progress in overcoming gaslighting. Reflect on the strategies you've been using to assert your own reality and protect yourself from manipulation. Celebrate your successes and identify any areas where you still feel vulnerable or uncertain. Use this time to set new goals and intentions for the month ahead, focusing on further strengthening your resilience against gaslighting tactics.

Verbal Abuse

Verbal abuse is a form of manipulation characterized by using words to control, belittle, or intimidate others. It can take various forms, including yelling, insults, threats, gaslighting, and humiliation. Verbal abusers often aim to undermine the confidence and self-worth of their victims, exerting power and control over them through verbal means.

This is quite common in romantic relationships. Some of us come off as partners who constantly criticize and demean our significant others, making hurtful comments about their appearance, intelligence, or abilities. For instance, we might say things like, "You're so stupid, you can't do anything right," or, "No one else would want you; you're lucky to have me." These hurtful words can leave the victim feeling ashamed, insecure, and trapped in an abusive relationship.

Overcoming verbal abuse tendencies requires us to put effort mainly into active listening and being empathetic.

Empathetic Listening—Listen attentively. When communicating with others, practice empathetic listening by truly focusing on understanding their perspective rather than formulating your response. As Stephen Covey wisely said, "Most people do not listen with the intent to understand; they listen with the intent to reply." Often, when we engage in verbal abuse or toxic communication, we're more concerned with asserting our own viewpoint than truly understanding the other person's. We're like loaded guns, ready to fire off our response without considering the impact. It's crucial to listen without projecting our own thoughts onto the speaker's words and instead seek to understand them as someone with unique experiences and perspectives. As Covey advises, "Seek first to understand, then to be understood."

Lying

Lying is a familiar concept to us all. At some point in our lives, we've likely resorted to telling a lie to protect ourselves or gain an advantage. However, it's important to recognize that lying is inherently harmful, especially when used to manipulate or deceive others.

When you're lying, you may fabricate stories, exaggerate details, or conceal facts to manipulate the perceptions or actions of others.

Recognizing when you're lying can be challenging, as it often involves deceiving yourself as well as others. However, some signs that you may be lying include avoiding eye contact, hesitating or stuttering while speaking, contradicting yourself, or displaying nervous body language such as fidgeting or sweating.

Lying can have serious consequences for both the liar and the individuals affected by the deception. It erodes trust and credibility in relationships, undermines honest communication, and damages the integrity of interpersonal interactions. When someone discovers that they have been lied to, they may feel betrayed, hurt, and resentful, leading to strained relationships and emotional distress.

For example, imagine a situation where a coworker asks you for feedback on their project, and you falsely praise their work to avoid conflict or confrontation. By lying about the quality of their project, you manipulate their perception and potentially hinder their growth and improvement opportunities. You may assume that by lying, you are protecting their feelings, but instead, your dishonesty damages trust and authenticity in your professional relationship, creating tension and resentment between you and your coworker.

The problem with lying is that the more you do it, the easier it becomes. You start to lose touch with the truth, and breaking free from this cycle requires double the effort. It's like a cancer that keeps spreading if left unchecked. Someone once told me that it's easier to tell another lie than to stop lying altogether.

First, it's important to acknowledge that overcoming lying tendencies won't happen overnight. You may find yourself slipping back into old habits along the way, but with determination and a genuine desire to change, it's possible to let go of this toxic behavior.

Here's how you can start:

- **Acknowledge the problem**. Admit to yourself that lying has become a problem and recognize the negative impact it's having on your life and relationships.
- **Identify triggers**. Pay attention to the situations or emotions that typically lead you to lie. This awareness will help you anticipate and address these triggers more effectively in the future.

- **Practice radical honesty**. Make a commitment to be completely honest, even when it's uncomfortable or difficult. Start by being truthful in small, everyday situations, and gradually work your way up to more challenging scenarios.
- **Challenge distorted thinking**. Question the beliefs or rationalizations that justify your lying behavior. Are you lying to avoid conflict, gain approval, or protect yourself from consequences? Recognize that these are often distorted thoughts and challenge them with rational, honest perspectives.
- **Seek support**. Don't hesitate to reach out to friends, family members, or a therapist for support and guidance on your journey to honesty. Having someone hold you accountable and provide encouragement can make a significant difference.
- **Practice self-compassion**. Be kind to yourself throughout this process. Understand that breaking free from lying habits is a journey, and it's okay to stumble along the way. Treat yourself with compassion and patience as you work toward positive change.

Withholding Affection or Sex

Picture this—you're in a relationship, and everything seems fine, but suddenly, your partner starts holding back on the hugs, kisses, and intimacy. They might even use it as a weapon, like saying, "You didn't do the dishes, so no cuddles for you tonight!" That's what we're dealing with here.

Now, recognizing when you're doing it can be a bit tricky. Are you avoiding physical closeness because you're genuinely not in the mood, or are you using it as a way to punish or manipulate your partner? If you find yourself using affection or sex as leverage to get what you want or to control the situation, then you might be guilty of this manipulative behavior.

Let's say your partner forgets to do something you asked them to do. Instead of talking it out like adults, you decide to give them the cold shoulder and withhold physical affection as a form of punishment. Not cool, right?

When you withhold affection or sex, it can make your partner feel rejected, unloved, and unwanted. Imagine if someone you care about suddenly stops hugging you, kissing you, or being intimate with you. It's like a punch to the gut, right? Your partner might start questioning themselves, wondering if they've done something wrong or if you've lost interest in them.

This behavior can also create distance and resentment in the relationship. Your partner might feel like they're walking on eggshells, afraid to upset you or do anything that might trigger another bout of affection withholding. Over time, this can erode trust and intimacy, leading to serious problems in the relationship.

So, while it might seem like a harmless way to get your point across or punish your partner, withholding affection or sex can cause a lot of harm and strain in your relationship. It's important to address any issues or concerns openly and honestly rather than resort to manipulative tactics.

Fortunately, I've discovered an amazing strategy that I've personally tested and found to be highly effective. By following these steps, you can begin to cultivate a healthier and more fulfilling relationship with your partner.

1. **Reflect on your motives**. Take some time to reflect on why you're withholding affection or sex from your partner. Are you doing it to manipulate them or punish them for something? Are there underlying issues in the relationship that need to be addressed?

2. **Communicate openly**. Instead of resorting to manipulative tactics, have an open and honest conversation with your partner about how you're feeling. Express your concerns or frustrations in a constructive way and listen to their perspective as well.

3. **Practice empathy**. Put yourself in your partner's shoes and try to understand how they might be feeling when you withhold affection or sex. Empathy can help you see the impact of your behavior on them and motivate you to make positive changes.

4. **Make a commitment to change**. Finally, commit to making positive changes in your behavior. This might involve setting boundaries, practicing better communication skills, or prioritizing your partner's emotional needs. Remember that change takes time and effort, but it's worth it for the health and happiness of your relationship.

Love Bombing

Love bombing is when someone showers you with excessive affection, attention, and gifts at the beginning of a relationship to manipulate you into thinking they're the best thing since sliced bread.

We've all heard those stories where someone's partner was all sunshine and rainbows at the beginning, but now they barely recognize them. It's like they went from being cheesy and nice to downright distant and cold. But here's the kicker —love bombing isn't just reserved for romantic relationships. It can happen anywhere, from friendships to professional settings.

So, are you the love-bombing type? How can you even tell if you're exhibiting this toxic behavior? Let's talk about it. I remember chatting with Samantha about why so many relationships seem to crash and burn because of love-bombing tendencies. Here's what she had to say: "You know, love bombing seems all good and sparkly at first. Sometimes, we might not even realize we're manipulating the other person. Take my ex, Luke, for example. When we first got together, I showered him with affection and support. He adored me and fell head over heels. But a few months into our relationship, I started slacking off on those things. He tried to bring it up, but I brushed it off every time. I didn't realize how bad things had gotten until he walked away. It hit me that I'd manipulated him into falling for a version of me that I couldn't keep up with. If I had just been genuine from the start, maybe he would have seen me for who I truly was. It stung, and I know he's the one that got away." It's like introducing a vibe you can't sustain.

I understand how tricky it is to overcome this behavior; however, here's a step-by-step approach you can start implementing today:

1. **Self-reflect**. Take some time to reflect on your past relationships and interactions. Think about instances where you may have gone overboard with affection or promises early on. Be honest with yourself about whether this behavior was genuine or if it was driven by a desire to win someone over.

2. **Set boundaries**. Establish clear boundaries for yourself when it comes to expressing affection and making promises. Avoid going overboard in the early stages of a relationship or friendship. Pace yourself and allow the other person to get to know the real you gradually.

3. **Focus on genuine connection**. Instead of showering someone with grand gestures or excessive compliments, focus on building a genuine connection. Invest time in getting to know the other person on a deeper level and allow the relationship to develop naturally over time.

4. **Communicate openly**. Be transparent about your feelings and intentions from the start. Avoid making unrealistic promises or commitments that you may struggle to keep in the long run. Honesty and open communication are key to building trust and fostering healthy relationships.

5. **Practice patience.** Remember that genuine relationships take time to develop. Avoid rushing into things or trying to force a connection. Allow the other person to set the pace and be patient as you navigate the journey together.

Guilt Tripping

Guilt tripping is when someone uses emotional manipulation to make others feel guilty for their actions or decisions.

Growing up with siblings often involves moments of guilt-tripping. I remember when my younger sister would constantly guilt-trip me into doing her chores by reminding me of the times I had borrowed her belongings without asking. For example, she would say, "I can't believe you won't help me with this when I let you borrow my bike last week!" It felt like emotional blackmail, with each of us trying to outmaneuver the other to avoid our own responsibilities. These experiences taught me how guilt-tripping can become ingrained in our behavior and how damaging it can be to relationships.

Here are some signs to look out for if you want to recognize if you possess this toxic trait:

- If we find ourselves using phrases like, "If you loved me, you would . . ." or, "I sacrificed so much for you," to get our way, we may be guilt-tripping.
- We feel entitled to other people's time, attention,

or resources and use guilt to coerce them into complying.

To overcome this behavior, the strongest weapon you need is empathy. It's about stepping outside of your own feelings and experiences and truly putting yourself in the other person's shoes. Consider what they might be going through, what their fears and concerns are, and how your actions or words might impact them.

Empathy allows you to recognize that everyone has their own boundaries and limitations. Just as you have your own needs and boundaries, so do others. Understanding this helps you realize that pushing someone beyond their limits or making them feel guilty for having boundaries is not fair or respectful.

Imagine you have a friend who often cancels plans at the last minute. Instead of immediately feeling hurt or angry, try to empathize with them. Consider that they might be dealing with stress at work or struggling with their mental health. Instead of guilt-tripping them or making them feel bad for canceling, you could reach out with understanding and support.

You might say something like, "Hey, I noticed you've been canceling plans a lot lately. Is everything okay? I'm here if you need someone to talk to or if you just need some time for yourself." This approach shows empathy and compassion, allowing your friend to feel supported without feeling guilty for their actions. It opens up a space for honest communication and strengthens your relationship based on mutual respect and understanding.

When you empathize with others, you acknowledge their humanity and recognize that they are entitled to their own thoughts, feelings, and decisions. This shift in perspective can be incredibly powerful in breaking the cycle of guilt-tripping and fostering healthier, more authentic relationships.

MANIPULATIVE BEHAVIOR SELF-ASSESSMENT

This checklist is designed to help you reflect on your behavior and identify any manipulative tendencies you may have. By honestly answering the questions below, you can gain insight into your actions and take steps toward healthier relationships.

1. Do you often find yourself trying to control others' decisions or actions?
2. Have you ever made someone feel guilty for not doing what you wanted?
3. Do you frequently use flattery or compliments to get your way?
4. Have you ever lied to manipulate a situation or avoid consequences?
5. Do you tend to avoid taking responsibility for your actions?
6. Have you ever threatened someone to get what you want?

7. Do you frequently withhold affection or attention to manipulate others?

8. Have you ever used emotional manipulation, such as playing the victim, to gain sympathy or support?

9. Do you often pressure others into doing things they are uncomfortable with?

10. Have you ever ignored someone to punish them or make them feel bad?

As we move forward, I understand that some of you may be feeling a bit uncomfortable or even called out after recognizing your behavior in this chapter. It's important to acknowledge that these behaviors are incredibly common and often manifest in both subtle and obvious ways. By highlighting various examples, my aim is to show that it's not always easy to recognize when we're being toxic and that many of us are in the same boat, learning and growing along the way. Remember, even the smallest efforts to change can make a big difference in how we connect with those who matter most to us. So take heart in knowing that you're not alone. With dedication and self-awareness, you can make meaningful strides toward building healthier relationships.

Now, as we journey forward, the next chapter offers a beacon of hope in repairing and nurturing relationships that may have been strained by toxic behavior. Through insightful guidance and practical tips, we'll explore ways to mend the bonds we value most and foster genuine connections built on trust, respect, and understanding.

CHAPTER 7

NURTURING HEARTFELT TIES

Nathan is the kind of guy who means well, but sometimes, his good intentions end up backfiring in the most spectacularly disastrous ways. Take, for example, his recent attempt at organizing a surprise birthday party for his best friend, Alex.

Nathan had been planning this for weeks, secretly coordinating with Alex's friends and family to pull off the ultimate surprise. But here's where things went off the rails. Instead of keeping the party under wraps, Nathan couldn't resist dropping hints left and right. He'd casually mention things like, "Hey, wouldn't it be wild if we threw a surprise party?" or, "I wonder what Alex's face would look like if we all jumped out and yelled 'Surprise!'"

Imagine Alex's dismay when he discovered that his so-called surprise party was anything but surprising. Thanks to Nathan's not-so-subtle hints, the element of surprise was as nonexistent as Nathan's poker face.

But that's just the tip of the iceberg when it comes to Nathan's accidental knack for toxic behavior. He has a habit of offering unsolicited advice. Recently, his friend Maya was venting about a tough day at work, and instead of simply listening, Nathan jumped in with a laundry list of suggestions on how to fix her problems. "You should have done this," or, "Why didn't you try that?" he'd say, completely missing the mark on what Maya really needed— a sympathetic ear, not a one-man advice column.

And then there's his penchant for making jokes at other people's expense. Nathan's quick wit and sharp tongue often land him in hot water, as his attempts at humor sometimes cross the line from funny to downright hurtful. He'll crack a joke about someone's appearance or poke fun at their insecurities, completely oblivious to the sting his words leave behind.

Now, before you go thinking Nathan's some kind of irredeemable individual, let me assure you—he's not. In fact, he's genuinely remorseful when he realizes the havoc his actions have wrought. It's just that sometimes, Nathan's good intentions get lost in translation, leaving a trail of hurt feelings and bruised egos in their wake.

This chapter offers us a chance to confront the harsh reality that our behaviors, however unintentional, can wreak havoc on the beautiful relationships we hold dear. It's about acknowledging that we've stumbled—maybe even fallen flat on our faces—but refuse to stay down.

LEARN HOW TO APOLOGIZE

In any moral framework, the right thing to do is apologize when we wrong others, especially if our intention is to preserve the relationship between us and those we have hurt. Unfortunately, many of us struggle to apologize effectively. Let's be honest—when we wrong others, we often just say, "I'm sorry," and we expect things to magically be okay again. But here's the truth—that's where we fall short because we don't fully understand the parameters of apologizing.

Did you know that different people have different apology languages? Maybe you're hearing about this concept for the first time. Well, imagine you accidentally spill coffee on your friend's favorite shirt. You might think a quick "I'm sorry" will suffice, but your friend might not feel truly apologized to unless you take further action, like offering to replace the shirt or sincerely expressing regret for ruining it.

Understanding apology languages can revolutionize the way we mend relationships. Here are some of the proven ways to apologize:

Express regret. Some people value hearing a genuine expression of remorse. To them, a heartfelt "I'm really sorry for what I did" goes a long way. For example, if you accidentally forget a friend's birthday, acknowledging your mistake and expressing genuine regret can show them that you care about their feelings.

Accept responsibility. Taking ownership of our actions is crucial in an apology. Saying something like, "I messed up, and I take full responsibility for my actions," demonstrates accountability. If you inadvertently cancel plans with a loved one at the last minute, acknowledging your fault and accepting responsibility can help rebuild trust.

Make restitution. Sometimes, actions speak louder than words. Offering to make things right or providing compensation can be an essential part of apologizing for some people. For instance, if you have been spreading rumors about a colleague, causing harm to their reputation and relationships in the workplace, making restitution could involve publicly acknowledging the falsehood of the rumors, apologizing to the colleague affected, and taking concrete steps to repair any damage caused.

Request forgiveness. Asking for forgiveness can be powerful in an apology. Saying, "I understand if you're upset, but I hope you can forgive me," acknowledges the hurt you've caused and expresses a desire to move forward positively. If you unintentionally offend a family member, asking for their forgiveness can pave the way for reconciliation.

Constructing a Meaningful Apology

A meaningful apology takes certain steps and is not just a plain "I'm sorry."

It's important to start by acknowledging your actions and expressing genuine remorse for the hurt you've caused. For example, "I want to apologize sincerely for my behavior. I realize now that my words and actions were hurtful, and I deeply regret causing you pain."

Once you have acknowledged your actions, take ownership of them without making excuses or shifting blame. Be honest about your role in the situation. For instance, "I take full responsibility for what I said and did. It was insensitive and wrong, and I am truly sorry."

Taking ownership is not all—you need to offer to make things right or provide restitution if possible. This could involve offering a solution to rectify the situation or compensate for any harm done. For example, "I understand that my actions have hurt you, and I want to make it up to you. Is there anything I can do to repair the damage or make you feel better?"

I vividly remember a time when I gaslit my friend, causing them to feel terrible about themselves, all to justify my actions. It was during a period when I was actively striving to better myself. After some deep self-reflection, I approached them and expressed my desire to talk things through, and they reluctantly agreed to have the conversation.

I recognized that I had wronged them on multiple occasions, and I understood that my apology might have seemed insincere, given the frequency of my mistakes. However, this time, I was determined to approach things differently. It wasn't just about uttering the words, "I'm sorry," but rather about assuring them of my sincere commitment to change my behavior and avoid repeating similar mistakes in the future.

Here is what I said: "I know I wronged you, and I made you feel bad about yourself to try and justify my behavior, but I'm really sorry, and I promise to work on myself and make sure this doesn't happen again. I value our friendship deeply, and I'm committed to being a better friend to you."

PRACTICING EMPATHY

Empathy means understanding how someone else feels and sharing their feelings. It's like putting yourself in their shoes and seeing things from their perspective.

Using empathy is crucial in repairing strained relationships caused by our behavior. When we empathize with others, we show them that we care about their feelings and understand the impact of our actions on them. This helps to rebuild trust and strengthen the connection between us. Empathy allows us to communicate more effectively, resolve conflicts peacefully, and ultimately, mend the bonds we value.

It's common advice to practice empathy, but let's be real—it's not always easy. We all have our own struggles and challenges to deal with in life. Now, being empathetic means not only dealing with our own stuff but also putting ourselves in the shoes of another person and seeing things from their perspective. And honestly, that can be a lot to handle.

But here's the thing—even though it's tough, it's the right thing to do, especially after our toxic behavior has hurt someone else. When we've caused pain or damage, it's essential to step into the other person's shoes and understand how our actions affected them. It's about acknowledging their feelings, even if it's uncomfortable or difficult for us. That's the first step toward making things right and rebuilding the trust and connection that may have been damaged. So, while it may not be easy, it's necessary to practice empathy, especially in repairing relationships affected by our behavior.

Practicing empathy is a systematic action that calls you to follow particular steps.

When someone is sharing their feelings or experiences with you, focus on truly listening without interrupting or judging. Give them your full attention, maintain eye contact, and nod or provide verbal cues to show that you're engaged. For example, if your friend is talking about a recent argument, you could say, "I understand," or, "That sounds really frustrating."

Try to imagine what the other person is feeling and why they might be feeling that way. Consider their perspective and background to gain a deeper understanding of their emotions. For instance, if your colleague seems stressed about a project deadline, think about the pressure they might be under and how it's affecting them.

Encourage the other person to share more about their feelings or experiences by asking open-ended questions. These questions invite them to express themselves more fully and help you gain insight into their perspective.

Instead of asking, "Are you okay?" which could prompt a simple yes or no answer, try asking, "How are you feeling about everything that's been happening?"

Let the other person know that you understand and accept their emotions, even if you don't necessarily agree with their perspective. Show empathy by acknowledging their feelings as valid and important. For example, you could say, "It sounds like you're really frustrated, and that's completely understandable given the circumstances."

After listening to the other person's perspective, take a moment to reflect on what they've shared before responding. Avoid jumping to conclusions or offering advice right away. Instead, respond with empathy and compassion, acknowledging their feelings and offering support if needed. You might say, "Thank you for sharing your thoughts with me. I can see why you feel that way, and I'm here to support you."

Now, I understand this may seem quite challenging and initially require a lot of effort. Incorporating empathy into your daily routine may feel like learning a new skill or breaking old habits. However, the more you practice and integrate it into your interactions, the more natural it becomes. Over time, empathy can evolve from a conscious effort into a deeply ingrained part of who you are. As you consistently choose empathy over toxic behaviors, you'll find that it not only strengthens your relationships but also shapes your character for the better.

REBUILDING TRUST WITH OTHERS

It's undeniable that when our toxic behaviors harm those closest to us, trust often takes a serious blow. Rebuilding that trust isn't just about repairing the damage; it's about deciding whether the relationship is worth salvaging. From my own experiences, I've found that it's often easier to mend an old relationship than to forge a new one from scratch. For instance, if your perceived sense of humor is what portrays your toxicity and leads to a loss of trust, it might be tempting to think, "These people don't understand my sense of humor; I'll just find new friends who do." However, the reality is that building new relationships takes time and effort, and there's no guarantee that the same issues won't arise again. So, instead of abandoning those relationships, it's worth considering how to rebuild trust and strengthen those bonds, even if it means confronting uncomfortable truths about our own behavior.

Meet Linda, a vibrant and outgoing college student who was known for her infectious laughter and quick wit. Linda was a proud member of her sorority, where she found a close-knit group of friends who shared her love for late-night study sessions and weekend adventures.

However, Linda had a habit of using sarcasm as a defense mechanism, often making biting remarks disguised as jokes. While she thought she was being funny and witty, her sorority sisters started to feel uncomfortable around her. They began to avoid spending time with Linda, fearing that they would become the target of her sharp tongue.

One evening, during a sorority event, Linda's sarcastic remarks crossed a line, leaving one of her sisters feeling hurt and humiliated. Instead of apologizing and acknowledging her mistake, Linda brushed off the incident, claiming that her friend was being too sensitive.

As time passed, Linda's toxic behavior continued to strain her relationships within the sorority. Her once-close friends started to distance themselves from her, and Linda found herself isolated and lonely. Despite her initial reluctance to admit fault, Linda eventually realized the impact of her behavior on her friendships.

Linda reached out to me, seeking guidance on how to mend her fractured relationships with her sorority sisters. Understanding her predicament, I empathized with her, and we brainstormed a strategic plan to rebuild trust and restore her friendships. Here's how Linda navigated her way through this challenging situation.

First, Linda took responsibility for her actions and acknowledged the impact of her sarcastic remarks on her friend. She reached out to her friend personally and offered a sincere apology, expressing genuine remorse for her hurtful behavior. "I realize now that my sarcastic remarks during the sorority event were hurtful and crossed a line. I'm truly sorry for the pain I caused you with my insensitive comments. Please know that it was never my intention to humiliate or upset you."

Next, Linda committed to actively listening to her friend's feelings and perspectives without dismissing or minimizing them. She demonstrated empathy by putting herself in her friend's shoes, seeking to understand the pain she had caused.

Linda also made a conscious effort to change her behavior by refraining from making sarcastic remarks in the future, especially in situations where they could cause harm or offense. She practiced self-awareness and self-control, recognizing the importance of respecting boundaries and being mindful of how her words and actions could affect others.

Furthermore, Linda took proactive steps to rebuild trust by consistently demonstrating her reliability and integrity. She followed through on her promises, showed up for her friends when they needed her, and acted with honesty and transparency in her interactions.

When we embark on the journey of rebuilding trust in fractured relationships, it's crucial to recognize that it's not solely within our control. The willingness of the other party to trust us again plays a significant role. Rebuilding trust doesn't guarantee automatic acceptance from the other person. Some individuals may need time to heal because they've been deeply hurt, while others may want to ensure our sincerity before opening up again. Therefore, patience is key. We shouldn't rush them or expect immediate reconciliation. Instead, we should continue to demonstrate genuine efforts to be better partners or friends. With time, consistency, and sincerity, they may eventually come around.

REBUILDING TRUST ONE STEP AT A TIME

Apologizing sincerely is a crucial step in repairing relationships damaged by our actions. However, it's not always easy to know how to apologize effectively. That's why I've created this step-by-step checklist to guide you through the process of offering a heartfelt apology. By following these steps and ticking off each item on the list, you can demonstrate your genuine remorse and commitment to making amends.

1. **Acknowledge your mistake.** Recognize and accept responsibility for what you've done wrong.
2. **Express remorse.** Show genuine regret for the hurt or harm caused by your actions.
3. **Be specific.** Clearly articulate what you're apologizing for without making excuses or deflecting blame.
4. **Offer restitution.** If appropriate, offer to make amends or rectify the situation.
5. **Promise change.** Make a sincere commitment to learn from your mistakes and avoid similar behavior in the future.
6. **Listen actively.** Allow the other person to express their feelings and perspective without interruption.
7. **Validate their feelings.** Acknowledge the impact of your actions on the other person's emotions.
8. **Ask for forgiveness.** Humbly request forgiveness and understand that it's ultimately up to the other person to grant it.

9. **Give them time**. Understand that healing takes time and respect the other person's need for space or forgiveness on their own terms.
10. **Follow up**. Check in with the person after some time has passed to show that you're still committed to repairing the relationship.

As we reflect on the insights shared in this chapter, it's essential to internalize them in a way that resonates with our own experiences. Each of us may have encountered moments where our toxic behaviors have strained relationships, causing pain and distance. However, through these personal anecdotes, we've gained a deeper understanding of the importance of self-awareness, empathy, and a genuine apology in repairing these bonds.

For me, it's been a journey of self-discovery, recognizing the patterns of behavior that have led to hurt and misunderstanding in my relationships. It's about acknowledging the times when I've faltered, owning up to my mistakes, and committing to doing better. Learning to apologize sincerely, empathize with others, and patiently rebuild trust has been transformative.

As we move forward, let's carry these lessons with us, not as abstract concepts but as tangible tools to navigate the complexities of our relationships. By applying them in our daily interactions, we can foster deeper connections, mend fractured ties, and cultivate a more fulfilling sense of community and belonging. Now, armed with insights gained from nurturing heartfelt ties, we're ready to take the next step toward fostering genuine connections. As we transition into our next chapter, "Cultivating Positive Conversations," let's harness the lessons learned and embark on a journey of constructive dialogue and mutual understanding.

CHAPTER 8
CULTIVATING POSITIVE CONVERSATIONS

Emma and Stacey were esteemed colleagues at a prestigious law firm and were known for their unwavering professionalism and impeccable work ethic. Their partnership was the envy of the office, characterized by seamless collaboration and impressive victories in the courtroom. However, even in the most esteemed environments, toxic communication patterns can erode the strongest of bonds.

Their rift began with a casual disagreement over an approach to a high-stakes case. Emma advocated for a meticulous and methodical strategy, emphasizing the importance of thorough research and preparation. Stacey, on the other hand, favored a bold and aggressive approach, believing that swift action and assertiveness were key to success.

As their conflicting viewpoints clashed, discussions turned into heated debates, and professional disagreements escalated into personal grievances. Tensions simmered beneath the surface, leading to misunderstandings, strained interactions, and a palpable sense of discord in the office.

This chapter serves as a guide for navigating the complexities of workplace relationships and beyond. By embracing the principles of positive communication, we can learn to avoid the pitfalls that Stacey and Emma encountered. Whether interacting with coworkers, bosses, partners, or friends, mastering these principles allows us to transform dynamics, mitigate conflicts, and foster thriving professional and personal relationships. It's about recognizing our own toxic communication habits and actively working to break them, thus safeguarding the vitality of our connections.

TOP TOXIC COMMUNICATION HABITS (AND HOW TO OVERCOME THEM)

It's no secret that effective communication is the cornerstone of healthy relationships. Yet, despite its importance, many of us struggle to communicate effectively, leading to numerous failed relationships and unresolved conflicts. But what lies at the heart of these communication breakdowns? The answer often lies in our toxic communication habits.

Getting Too Defensive

Getting too defensive is a common communication habit that can damage relationships. If you tend to feel the need to justify yourself excessively, react angrily to criticism, and shift blame onto others, it is a sign of defensiveness. This behavior is damaging because it shuts down communication, prevents understanding, and undermines trust. For example, during a disagreement, instead of listening to your partner's concerns about household chores, you immediately become defensive and list all the times you've helped in the past. To stop being defensive, pause and reflect before responding, actively listen to the other person's perspective, own your mistakes, and communicate openly using "I" statements.

Using Frustrated Language

Using frustrated language is another toxic communication habit that can harm relationships. We all get stressed and work on different things, but when we start using aggressive or confrontational language, raising our voices, and making sweeping statements, we are simply being toxic. This escalates conflicts, hurts feelings, and erodes trust and respect. For instance, during a conversation about forgetfulness, you might say, "You always forget important things! It's like you don't care about anything except yourself." To avoid using frustrated language, stay calm, use neutral language, and seek clarification when needed.

Being Too Critical

Being too critical of your partner can chip away at their self-esteem and create resentment in the relationship. When you are too critical, you constantly find fault with your partner, nitpick their actions, and make derogatory comments. This behavior erodes trust, fosters insecurity, and creates a hostile environment. For instance, if your partner forgets to buy groceries, you might respond by saying, "You never remember anything! You're so unreliable." To stop being too critical, focus on constructive feedback, praise your partner's efforts, and choose your words carefully.

Using Negative Body Language

Using negative body language, such as eye-rolling, crossing your arms, or avoiding eye contact, can convey hostility, disinterest, and disrespect in communication. Tendencies of negative body language include avoiding physical touch, fidgeting, and maintaining a tense posture during conversations with your partner. When you do this, you create barriers to understanding, escalate conflicts, and hinder emotional connection. A colleague, Marietta, shared that she doesn't know how to talk to Phil, her partner, about finances anymore because each time she brings up the topic, he starts to sigh loudly, signaling impatience or contempt. To overcome this, she should maintain open and relaxed body language and express empathy through nonverbal cues like nodding and smiling.

Steamrolling Your Partner

Steamrolling your partner is when one person dominates conversations, disregards their partner's input, and imposes their own opinions or decisions. This is quite common, and I bet many of us have found ourselves in such situations, whether we are the ones steamrolling or being steamrolled.

Do you constantly interrupt your partner, dismiss their ideas, and insist on having the final say in every discussion? Well, I have news for you—you are toxic at communication. I vividly recall an incident from a couple of years ago during a work retreat involving a prominent couple, Anne and Paul. Anne, being vocal and assertive, contrasted sharply with Paul's more reserved nature, yet they appeared deeply connected. During a group activity, Paul was asked what he would do if he won the lottery. Before Paul could respond, Anne jumped in, confidently stating, "He would definitely buy a Porsche and a beach house." However, Paul surprised everyone by expressing his actual desire to invest in unit trust funds and stock markets. This behavior suppresses your partner's voice, breeds resentment, and diminishes trust in the relationship. To refrain from steamrolling, give your partner space to express themselves, and be open to compromise and collaboration.

Assuming Your Partner Already Knows

The year is 2024, and to date, most of us have failed to learn that to be understood, we must be able to communicate clearly and openly. Yet, we often fall into the trap of assuming that our partners can intuitively grasp our thoughts, feelings, or needs without us articulating them. It's a common misconception rooted in the desire to believe that our partners know us well enough and value our relationship enough to understand our wants and needs without explicit communication.

However, the reality is quite different. Expecting someone to always read you correctly sets both parties up for disappointment. Your partner, no matter how much they love you, is human and won't always be able to anticipate your desires accurately. After all, nobody is that good a guesser. It doesn't mean they love you any less. Think about it—wouldn't it be way more meaningful if you told your partner exactly what you like, want, need, or expect and watched them follow through because they listened to you rather than guessed what you want and most likely got it wrong?

For example, if you're upset with your partner for forgetting an important date in your relationship, the solution is not to go rogue and cut communication with them. Perhaps they forgot about the date because they are rather busy or have something going on. To overcome this form of behavior, practice clear and direct communication, express your needs and expectations explicitly, and encourage your partner to do the same.

Stonewalling

There should be a Nobel Prize for the person who started this kind of behavior because they successfully came up with one of the most toxic and damaging forms of communication mankind can conjure. Stonewalling and giving someone the silent treatment are destructive communication behaviors when one partner withdraws from interaction, refuses to engage in conversation, or ignores the other person as a way to avoid conflict or punish them. This behavior pushes us to shut down emotionally, refuse to communicate with or respond to our partners, and physically leave or avoid situations where communication is needed. For example, if your partner confronts you about an issue and you respond by completely ignoring them or walking away without a word, you're employing stonewalling tactics. To stop stonewalling and giving silent treatment, practice active listening, express your feelings and concerns calmly and assertively, and commit to resolving conflicts through open and respectful communication.

There's a significant difference between needing a moment to process your emotions and shutting down communication entirely.

Taking time to collect your thoughts can be a healthy response to escalating conflicts. It allows you to cool off and approach the conversation with a clearer mind, reducing the risk of saying something hurtful in the heat of the moment. However, the important thing to do is to let your partner know that you need some time. Communicate calmly and respectfully, saying that you cannot discuss the matter immediately and need some time to think things over. This ensures transparency and prevents your partner from feeling ignored or shut out.

It's vital to follow through on your commitment to revisit the conversation after you've had time to process it. Ignoring the issue indefinitely or using "I need time" to avoid discussing uncomfortable topics altogether can lead to further misunderstandings and resentment.

HOW TO TALK ABOUT YOUR TRAUMA WITH YOUR LOVED ONES

Communication breakdowns often occur because we tend to suppress our emotions and true feelings when confronted with traumatic events in our lives. Trauma has a profound impact, altering our thoughts, reasoning, reactions, and emotions. Yet, when we choose to deal with it without involving those close to us, it gradually erodes our well-being. Many of us, especially men, fear that discussing our pain will be perceived as a sign of weakness, which is a harmful misconception.

In my years of experience, I have learned that to be able to speak about your trauma, you need to accept it, own it, and be comfortable with yourself. The moment you are not, it is going to be hard to open up about it. Recently, I met with an old acquaintance, Laura, over lunch, and during our conversation, she seemed hesitant and withdrawn. Eventually, she confided in me about a traumatic experience she had endured—a violent mugging that left her shaken and fearful. Laura admitted that she had struggled to come to terms with the incident, often avoiding discussing it with others because it brought up feelings of vulnerability and fear. She expressed her reluctance to open up about the trauma, fearing judgment or disbelief from others.

Once you're comfortable with your traumatic experience, planning what you will say can help you express yourself more clearly and confidently. Staying calm is crucial during these conversations. Let's say you and your partner have had a joint savings account for future investments, and, unfortunately, you've been scammed out of all your investment savings. It can be incredibly hard to talk about this with your partner.

You may start by saying, "I have been meaning to talk to you about this for quite some time, and I apologize for not bringing it up earlier. I didn't know how to broach the subject because I was still processing the shock and devastation of what happened. However, I now feel that I'm emotionally in a better place to discuss it with you."

Establishing trust is fundamental when discussing your trauma with loved ones. It creates a safe space for open and honest communication, allowing both parties to feel heard and supported. To build trust, reassure your loved one that you value their support and that you trust them with your vulnerability.

For example, you could say something like, "I want you to know how much I value our relationship and your support. It's difficult for me to talk about what happened, but I trust you enough to share this with you. I hope that by opening up, we can strengthen our bond and navigate through this together."

Acknowledging how the trauma affects you is an essential step in the conversation. It allows your loved one to understand the impact it has had on you emotionally, mentally, and physically. Expressing your feelings validates your experience and helps your loved one empathize with what you're going through.

You might say, "I want to share with you how this experience has been affecting me. It's been incredibly challenging to cope with the emotions and thoughts that come up. I've been feeling (describe your emotions, such as anxious, overwhelmed, or sad), and it's been taking a toll on my daily life. I hope that by sharing this with you, you can better understand what I'm going through and offer your support."

To keep the conversation going, encourage open dialogue and active listening. Allow your loved one to ask questions and share their thoughts and feelings without judgment. This creates a safe space for both of you to express yourselves honestly and openly.

Setting up mutual understanding involves validating each other's perspectives and feelings. Acknowledge any concerns or reactions your loved one may have and address them with empathy and compassion. Strive to find common ground and work together toward a shared understanding of the situation.

For example, you could say, "I appreciate your willingness to listen and understand what I'm going through. I understand that this may be difficult for you as well, and I want to make sure we're on the same page. Let's keep talking and supporting each other through this."

Remember, you have the right to control the pace and depth of the conversation about your trauma. You don't have to disclose anything you're not comfortable sharing. It's essential to prioritize your emotional well-being and boundaries throughout the discussion.

If you feel overwhelmed or triggered during the conversation, it's okay to take a break or redirect the discussion to a topic that feels safer for you. Communicate openly with your loved one about your needs and boundaries, and encourage them to respect your limits.

For example, you could say, "I appreciate your support and willingness to listen, but I'm feeling overwhelmed right now. Can we take a break and revisit this conversation later? I want to make sure I'm in the right headspace to discuss this further." This allows you to take care of yourself while still maintaining open communication with your loved one.

SET, REBUILD, AND COMMUNICATE HEALTHY BOUNDARIES

When most of us hear the word "boundaries," we often think of walls separating us from others, creating a sense of distance or isolation. However, boundaries are not about building barriers; rather, they are about establishing guidelines that promote healthy relationships. Healthy boundaries are like personal space markers that define where you end and where others begin. They serve as guidelines for how you want to be treated and how you will treat others, ensuring mutual respect, safety, and emotional well-being in relationships.

Setting boundaries can involve expressing your needs, preferences, and limits to your partner, friends, or family members. It's about clearly communicating what feels comfortable and acceptable to you and what doesn't. Boundaries can encompass various aspects of life, including physical, emotional, and interpersonal boundaries. They help maintain a balance between connection and autonomy, allowing individuals to preserve their sense of self while engaging in relationships with others.

Physical Boundaries—These are about your personal space and physical touch. For instance, you can set boundaries by letting someone know if you're comfortable with hugs or prefer to keep some distance. If a friend tends to invade your personal space, you might say, "I like my space, so let's keep a bit of distance, okay?"

Emotional Boundaries—These involve protecting your emotions and feelings. You can set emotional boundaries by expressing how you want to be treated during conversations. For example, if a friend constantly criticizes you, you can say, "I feel hurt when you criticize me. Can we focus on positive conversations instead?"

Time Boundaries—These are about managing your time and commitments. You can set boundaries by being clear about your availability and priorities. For instance, if a colleague asks you to work late, but you have plans, you can say, "I have plans tonight, but I can help first thing tomorrow morning."

Digital Boundaries—In today's digital age, it's essential to set boundaries around technology use. You can establish boundaries by setting limits on screen time or defining when it's appropriate to text or call. For example, you might say, "I prefer not to answer work emails after 7 p.m. Let's discuss it during office hours."

Healthy boundaries also require effective, respectful communication. You don't have to be rude or confrontational when expressing your boundaries. Instead, you can communicate them in a simple and respectful way that others will understand and respect.

Be clear and direct. Clearly state your boundaries without beating around the bush. For example, if you need some alone time, you can say, "I need some time to myself right now."

Use "I" statements. Take ownership of your feelings and needs by using "I" statements. For instance, instead of saying, "You always interrupt me," you can say, "I feel frustrated when I'm interrupted."

Be firm but polite. Firmly assert your boundaries while maintaining a polite tone. For example, if someone asks for a favor that you're not comfortable with, you can say, "I appreciate you asking, but I'm not able to help with that."

Offer alternatives. If possible, suggest alternatives that respect both your boundaries and the other person's needs. For instance, if someone wants to hang out when you're busy, you can say, "I'm not available tonight, but I'd love to catch up over lunch tomorrow."

Set consequences. If someone continues to disregard your boundaries, calmly communicate the consequences. For example, you can say, "If you keep texting me late at night, I'll need to silence my notifications."

HOW TO COMMUNICATE GENUINELY WITH OTHERS

Communication lies at the heart of many of our toxic behaviors, often stemming from our inability to communicate genuinely and respectfully. I firmly believe that by mastering the art of genuine and respectful communication, we can significantly reduce the prevalence of toxic habits in our interactions. It's through genuine communication that we can foster understanding, empathy, and mutual respect in our relationships.

Tone and Body Language

Checking your tone and body language is crucial in genuine communication. Your tone can convey as much, if not more, than your words, so it's essential to ensure it aligns with your message.

The tone you use can significantly impact the meaning of your message. Even the simplest statement can be perceived differently depending on the tone in which it's delivered. For example, saying, "Can you please pass the salt?" with a polite and friendly tone is more likely to be well-received than saying it with an impatient or demanding tone.

The importance of your message can be lost or diminished if delivered with the wrong tone. For instance, expressing sympathy for someone's loss with a cheerful or flippant tone can come across as insensitive and disrespectful.

Finding the right tone for the right message is crucial for effective communication. It involves being mindful of the emotions and sensitivities of the other person and adjusting your tone accordingly. For example, when offering constructive criticism, using a supportive and encouraging tone can make the feedback more constructive and easier to accept.

Similarly, your body language can either reinforce or contradict what you're saying. In the section about toxic communication habits, we realized that crossing your arms or avoiding eye contact may signal defensiveness or disinterest, even if your words suggest otherwise.

Be Real

Being real in communication means being genuine and sincere. It's about speaking from the heart and expressing your thoughts and feelings honestly. Instead of pretending to agree with someone just to avoid conflict, you can respectfully voice your differing opinions while still being considerate of their perspective. Authenticity fosters trust and deepens connections in relationships. You could say, "I understand where you're coming from, and I applaud the effort you have invested in this; however, regarding the recent events and available data, you are coming off wrong."

It's Not All about You

Remember that genuine communication isn't about you—it's about the other person. It involves actively listening to their needs, concerns, and emotions without making it about your own agenda or ego. For example, if a friend is sharing a personal struggle, resist the urge to turn the conversation back to yourself. Instead, focus on offering empathy and support without hijacking the spotlight.

Knowing how to be authentic means being true to yourself while also respecting others' boundaries and feelings. It's about finding the balance between expressing your authentic self and considering the impact of your words and actions on those around you. By practicing self-awareness and empathy, you can communicate authentically while nurturing positive and genuine connections with others.

HONING AUTHENTICITY

As Maya Angelou once wisely noted, "Authenticity is not something we have or don't have. It's a practice—a conscious choice of how we want to live." Authenticity often involves discovering methods to express your true self and aspiring to be a better person instead of allowing circumstances to dictate your actions. By mentally rehearsing situations beforehand, you can equip yourself to anticipate challenges and navigate them while staying aligned with your authentic self. Through visualization, you will tap into your inner resources and set intentions for future interactions. This exercise aims to empower you to communicate with honesty, empathy, and integrity, ultimately strengthening your ability to connect authentically with those around you.

- Take a moment to reflect on past conversations where you felt you weren't authentic or genuine.

What were the circumstances? How did you feel during and after the conversation?

- Consider the core values and principles that you want to uphold in your interactions with others. These values could include honesty, empathy, respect, and openness.
- Close your eyes and imagine a future conversation where you want to communicate authentically. Picture the setting, the person you're talking to, and the topic of discussion.
- Before starting the visualization, set intentions for the conversation. What do you hope to achieve? How do you want the other person to feel after the conversation? Visualize yourself expressing your thoughts and feelings authentically while maintaining respect and empathy.
- In your visualization, not only focus on how you speak but also on how you listen. Imagine yourself actively listening to the other person's perspective without judgment or interruption.
- As you visualize the conversation, pay attention to your emotions. Notice any feelings of discomfort, anxiety, or resistance that arise. Acknowledge these emotions and explore their underlying causes.
- If you encounter challenges or discomfort during the visualization, take note of them and consider how you can address them in future interactions. Repeat the visualization exercise regularly to reinforce your commitment to authenticity in communication.

- After visualizing future conversations, make a conscious effort to apply what you've visualized in real-life interactions. Practice speaking authentically, listening actively, and staying true to your values.
- Regularly reflect on your progress in practicing authenticity in communication. Notice any improvements in your relationships, increased trust and understanding, and personal growth.
- Don't hesitate to seek feedback from trusted friends or mentors on your communication style and authenticity. Their insights can provide valuable perspectives and help you continue to refine your approach.

LET OTHERS KNOW THAT TOXICITY CAN BE OVERCOME

You have seen that overcoming toxicity involves three main steps: knowing yourself, loving yourself, and building genuine relationships with others. The first two steps focus just on you, and the third is centered on your relationships with others. It is important to understand why you turned to toxic behaviors in the first place, so you can mend old hurts and commit to a healthier life for yourself and your loved ones. I hope you have already advanced quite far in your journey. If so, you're in the perfect position to help someone else, simply by sharing your thoughts with them.

IN UNDER 1 MINUTE
YOU CAN HELP OTHERS JUST LIKE YOU BY LEAVING A REVIEW!

Thanks for letting someone else know that toxicity does not define them. May you continue to let love for yourself and others lead the way. Scan the QR code:

CONCLUSION

As we reach the end of our journey together, it's important to reflect on the key messages and takeaways from our exploration of toxic behaviors and their antidotes. Throughout this book, we've gone into the depths of toxic habits and mindsets, examining insights, strategies, and practical tools to help you navigate the path toward positive change.

At its core, this book is a guide for those grappling with challenging behaviors and thought patterns. It's a reminder that transformation is possible, albeit not always easy or swift. By embracing the Anti-Toxic SSB System—self-awareness, self-love, and building genuine relationships—you've laid the foundation for meaningful change in your life and relationships.

First and foremost, self-awareness is the cornerstone of this journey. When you recognize and acknowledge your struggles without judgment, you lay the foundation for meaningful change. Self-awareness empowers you to understand your behaviors, motivations, and emotions, enabling you to navigate life's challenges with clarity and purpose.

Learning to love yourself is a transformative act that boosts self-esteem and self-respect. When you embrace self-love, you become more confident in setting boundaries and seeking to become the best version of yourself. Remember, you are worthy of love and respect, and embracing this truth will guide you toward a fulfilling life.

Equipped with the tools provided in this journey, you have the power to build genuine relationships with others. By mastering your communication habits and empathetically putting yourself in others' shoes, you'll draw people to you rather than push them away. Genuine connections are formed when we authentically engage with others, listening with empathy and speaking with sincerity.

All around us, people are communicating in all the wrong ways, including us. We are wired to think and act as we were raised, and having self-awareness and a desire to change is the first step. There is such a struggle to create lasting relationships that are truly genuine. How can we work through relationship problems if we haven't figured out the problems within ourselves? There is a huge need for guidance, both direct and empathetic, and I hope this book has contributed to filling that need.

My life is a testament to the power of self-awareness and how a desire to change can propel you into a journey you never would have set foot on had you not experienced some inner struggle. Whether you're a textbook narcissist or you simply have some toxic tendencies, I believe we all have default traits that we need to accept responsibility for and strive to change. Personal growth is my life's mission. I am living proof that change is possible, and I want others to know it and have the resources to make it a reality.

My motivation for this book comes directly from the relationships I am surrounded by—my family dynamic, my marriage, my friendships, my relationships with coworkers and mentors, and even my spiritual connections. While I was writing this book, a coworker vented to me about their marriage taking a turn for the worse due to their spouse's stonewalling responses to hard discussions and their inability to empathize with anything they say. A friend has struggled with breaking up with someone because their partner has emotionally manipulated them into staying, saying that if my friend left, they would become depressed. Another friend has kept a secret from their spouse because they're ashamed and afraid of disappointing them when they should be more afraid of how their spouse will feel when they find out they've been lying. I've been unfriended and called hurtful things on social media for simply disagreeing with a friend's opinion, as if disagreements are proper grounds to break ties (as we've learned, disagreements are opportunities to strengthen connections and understand each other better). The point is that toxic behavior patterns are prevalent in our surroundings. Recognizing them doesn't authorize us to pass judgment on others. Instead, these instances provide opportunities for self-reflection. They are chances to look inward and acknowledge areas where we can grow and develop if we approach these areas with sincerity.

As I come to the end of writing this journey, I'm delighted to share that some of those people have been actively working on their self-awareness and honesty. It's inspiring to witness them shedding their own bad habits, one step at a time. It serves as a powerful reminder that small changes can lead us in the right direction.

Stay committed to the journey and be excited for the moments of accomplishment, reconciliation, and true, raw connection that lie ahead. Your efforts will not go unnoticed, and with time, you'll experience the transformative power of genuine change.

I invite you to share your thoughts and experiences by leaving a review on Amazon. Your feedback not only helps others discover the benefits of this book but also fuels my continued efforts to support individuals like you on their journey toward positive change.

So, as you embark on the next chapter of your life, hold onto the lessons learned, the insights gained, and the tools acquired. Embrace the power of self-awareness, the strength of self-love, and the beauty of authentic relationships. Above all, believe in yourself and your capacity to create positive change.

REFERENCES

Betts, Jennifer L. . "100+ Self-Love Quotes to Uplift and Empower You." LoveToKnow. LoveToKnow Media, August 18, 2022. https://www.lovetoknow.com/quotes-quips/love/self-love-quotes.

Colan, Lee. "12 Quotes to Help You Build More Powerful Relationships." Inc. Mansueto Ventures, March 30, 2016. https://www.inc.com/lee-colan/12-quotes-to-help-you-build-more-powerful-relationships.html.

Gillihan, Seth. "What is Narcissism? Symptoms, Causes, Diagnosis, Treatment, and Prevention." EverydayHealth, December 20, 2022. https://www.everydayhealth.com/narcissism/

Green, Rachael. "Is Narcissism Genetic?" Verywell Mind, March 14, 2023. https://www.verywellmind.com/is-narcissism-genetic-7111210.

Indeed. "Finding Yourself Quotes (Including Importance and Tips)." November 27, 2022. https://ca.indeed.com/career-advice/career-development/finding-yourself-quotes

Jhangiani, Rajiv, and Hammond Tarry. "3.2 The Feeling Self: Self-Esteem," January 26, 2022. https://opentextbc.ca/socialpsychology/chapter/the-feeling-self-self-esteem/.

Menahem, Sam, and Melanie Love. "Forgiveness in Psychotherapy: The Key to Healing." *Journal of Clinical Psychology* 69, no. 8 (August 2013): 829–35. https://doi.org/10.1002/jclp.22018.

Mitra, Paroma, Tyler J. Torrico, and Dimy Fluyau. "Narcissistic Personality Disorder." In *StatPearls*. Treasure Island (FL): StatPearls Publishing, 2024. http://www.ncbi.nlm.nih.gov/books/NBK556001/.

Nash, Jo. "23 Post Traumatic Growth Worksheets for Therapy (+PDF)." PositivePsychology.com, November 20, 2019. https://positivepsychology.com/post-traumatic-growth-worksheets/.

Pickering, Gisèle, André Mazur, Marion Trousselard, Przemyslaw Bienkowski, Natalia Yaltsewa, Mohamed Amessou, Lionel Noah, and Etienne Pouteau. "Magnesium Status and Stress: The Vicious Circle Concept Revisited." *Nutrients* 12, no. 12 (November 28, 2020): 3672. https://doi.org/10.3390/nu12123672.

"Self Awareness Quotes (3530 Quotes)," n.d. https://www.goodreads.com/quotes/tag/self-awareness.

Sharma, Robin S. *The 5 AM Club: Own Your Morning, Elevate Your Life*. First edition. Toronto, Ontario, Canada: HarperCollins Publishers Ltd, 2018.

Young, Hayley A., and David Benton. "Heart-Rate Variability: A Biomarker to Study the Influence of Nutrition on Physiological and Psychological Health?" *Behavioural Pharmacology* 29, no. 2 and 3 (April 2018): 140–51. https://doi.org/10.1097/FBP.0000000000000383.